Working Man From Big Snowbird

Working Man From Big Snowbird

Marilyn Curtis Trull

iUniverse

WORKING MAN FROM BIG SNOWBIRD

iUniverse books may be ordered through booksellers or by contacting:

iUniverse
1663 Liberty Drive
Bloomington, IN 47403
www.iuniverse.com
1-800-Authors (1-800-288-4677)

Because of the dynamic nature of the Internet, any web addresses or links contained in this book may have changed since publication and may no longer be valid. The views expressed in this work are solely those of the author and do not necessarily reflect the views of the publisher, and the publisher hereby disclaims any responsibility for them.

Any people depicted in stock imagery provided by Thinkstock are models, and such images are being used for illustrative purposes only.
Certain stock imagery © Thinkstock.

ISBN: 978-1-5320-0030-0 (sc)
ISBN: 978-1-5320-0031-7 (e)

Library of Congress Control Number: 2016910818

Print information available on the last page.

iUniverse rev. date: 08/25/2016

Dedication

Jonathan Easton Trull,
infant son of Jon &
Crystal June 16th 2014

ACKNOWLEDGEMENTS

Roma Hedrick, Ted Hedrick, Minnie Jo Watts, Loyd Hedrick, Novella Hyde, Lennox Hedrick, Pat Williams, Jimtom Hedrick, Joy Dutcher, Tina Hopper, Jane Birchfield, Debra Pitcox Robinson, Connie Adams Gunter, these are people who shared their stories. I would like to thank my good friend, Toni Martin, who shared her writing experience and gave me so much encouragement. One of my good friends, Suzanne Van Gorder, gave me the information about her father, Dr. Van Gorder. I give special thanks to my son, Jon Trull for helping me navigate through all my computer problems I am constantly having, also for helping edit. Thank you to Karen Trull for special little stories. I want to give a big thank you to Stephanie Carpenter who reached out to help me to help edit this book while finishing her own book.

SPECIAL ACKNOWLEDGEMENTS FOR DIAMOND

The list of all the really special loggers are just going to be named. They were all loyal, hardworking, honest, and Diamond loves you all. Gary Jones, Gary Gregory, Charlie Hass, Dean Hass, Marvin Guffey, JD Guffey, Ronald Guffey, Chris Guffey, Paul Rose, Brian Rose, Carl Patterson, Eddie Duckett, Ronnie Robinson, Ronald Patterson, David Holder, Jamie Brooks, Edward Holder, John Byrd, Jim Byrd, Scotty Cope, Robert Winfrey, Denman Adams, Rance Adams, Terry Adams, Lonnie Underwood, Lonnie Stewart, Edward Holder, Robert Williams, Kyle Williams, Mathew Hyde, Mark Rogers, Chuck Stewart, Jeff Waldroup, Terry Buchanan, Wendell Waldroup, Sam Crisp, Sam Crisp Jr., Jessie Crisp, Tony Millsaps, Garfield Carringer, Steve Carpenter, Steve Curtis, Mike Curtis, Steve Jordan, Marty Moody, Joe Moody, Leonard Moody, Wade Moody, Dillard Moody, Lester Adams, Roger Adams, Arvil Adams, Kerry Don Adams, Lexter Stewart, Dennis Stewart, Red Eller, Joe Eller, Dustin Eller, Lum Cody, Bobbie Cody, Chuckie Cody, Greg Grindstaff, Doyle Grindstaff, Bobbie McGuire, Wayne McGuire, Josh McGuire, Lexter Adams, Harold Beasley, Bobbie Beasley, David Brooks, Mathew Williams, Harold Orr, Darrell Shope, Donnie Orr, Gary Buchanan, and Jimmy Smith. Diamond doesn't want to leave anyone out, if somehow he does, he didn't mean to overlook you, it's just hard to remember all the names.

CHAPTER ONE

Worst Deal He Ever Made

On May 7th, 1939, an unexpected cold snap hit the Snowbird Mountains. Jasper Hedrick's wife, Mary, was in her ninth month of pregnancy and on this night her time had come. The oldest son, Ted, took the younger brother, Lennox, and the younger sister, Minnie Jo, to Grandpa and Grandma Hedrick's to spend the night. The oldest daughter, Novella, stayed home to help her Mommy. Jasper sent for Mandy Thompson, the mid wife, to come and assist with the baby. Jasper then had to focus on cutting wood to build a fire to warm the house.

The new baby took all night and he was the most beautiful baby they had ever seen. He had the bluest eyes and his hair was a glistening blonde with silver threads through it. As Mary held him in the light of the coal oil lamp, he seemed to sparkle. She told Jasper she wanted to name him "Diamond." Jasper told her he really wanted to call him Albert. Mary said, "You can name him Albert, but I will call him Diamond." They named him Albert Diamond Hedrick and they called him DIAMOND. Jasper paid the midwife in can goods: one quart of beans, one quart of tomatoes, and one quart of corn. Jasper would later joke that it was the worst deal he ever made.

The Hedrick's were a very loving couple and very thankful for their many blessings. They had to work very hard for what they had, but they always took time for the sweet things in life. They would go out on the porch at night for some alone time after the kids were asleep. That was a quiet time when the work for the day was over. The Snowbird Mountains are such a peaceful place at night, nothing but the sounds of the whippoorwill, the peeper frogs, the katydids, or the sound of the screech owl. It was a time for planning the next day's chores that Jasper expected the children to get done. He laid the ground work, knowing Mary would accomplish it all in her sweet loving way. Mary was tender, but she always got results.

Every morning, Jasper geared up his horse and led him walking seven miles to Santeetlah. It was still so dark and most of the time he couldn't see where he was going. When the deep ruts were frozen hard, he would sometimes fall and get hurt badly. His hands would break open and bleed. All this for $2.50 a day for him and his horse.

As soon as he got home in the evening and ate his supper, he and one of the oldest children would head out over on the hillside to put up acid wood (pulp wood). All this to pay his boss, Lawrence Bemis, for the beautiful acreage he bought from him. Jasper was so sure he couldn't afford this large beautiful piece of property on Big Snowbird, but Lawrence said he would make sure he could. They met in the office one day and signed the papers. For $650.00 he bought 259 acres from gap to gap. Right after Lawrence Bemis signed, he took a dose of backing soda for indigestion and fell over dead with a heart attack.

The property was beautiful with so many water sources and fertile land for crops. Jasper had a vision of all his brothers and sisters to live close, so he would make sure they could afford theirs. You might say it became "Hedrickville." The land would become the home for Jasper's mother and father, Pose and Frieda Hedrick, as well as Jasper and Mary Hedrick. Also the families of Jasper's brothers Leslie, John, and Marvin, and sisters, Neter and Nettie.

The first things that Jasper would do to make a homestead was to put all the amenities in place to start a life. Before the house went up came the barn, corn crib, springhouse, and can house. These were a few of the things that had to come first. He then purchased lumber from Bemis Lumber Company to build their house. It was a wood shingled roof with rough lumber boards for the siding.

Mary had a long kitchen and the table was long as well, with a bench that was probably around eight feet long. That's where the little folks ate. On each end there was a chair where Jasper and Mary ate. There were chairs on the other side for the older kids. Everyone would hungrily sit down at their usual place, but nobody touched the food until Mary sat down, Jaspers rule!

Mary Hedrick was the fastest little woman in the kitchen. When Jasper's feet hit the floor, Mary's did, too. She cooked a big breakfast for Jasper and the kids, while at the same time she was making a lunch for Jasper. As soon as Jasper got off to work, she headed to the barn to milk two cows. Diamond always told his mommy he could never get the hang of milking, so he could get out of it. He would go with her and spray the cows for flies, just to be with her. He loved being close to his mommy. After the milking was complete, Mary would strain the milk and the kids would take it to the spring house.

Mary made wonderful treats for the family. Every morning she made fried apple pies and put them in Jasper's lunch box. They were really delicious! He would always, no matter how bad he wanted them, save one for the baby of the family. The baby would always meet him on his return from work a little ways up the road to get that pie. Diamond says he stayed the baby longer than any of them did. Three years later it was Loyd who met Dad. Then Roma came along about the time Moon

Pies came out in the stores. Jasper would put cheese in his and bring an extra one for Roma. Diamond didn't mind Roma at all, he loved his little baby sister. He had resented Loyd from the time he was born, until he got big enough to play with him.

Mary had many old country recipes that were handed down from her mother and grandmothers. They came from times when you lived off the land. She would put a little grease and sugar in a large black iron skillet and fry blackberries that she and the kids were always picking. She always told the kids they had to fry until they made that certain popping noise. She made biscuits every day and when she was in a hurry she made biscuit bread. It was also made in a big black skillet and it was called "Johnny cake." All of the biscuits and streaked meat that were left over at breakfast went into the warming cabinet. When the hungry little kids got off the school bus, they headed for Mommy's warming cabinet. After a quick snack from the cabinet the children had to get on their chores. Diamond's job was carrying in the many loads of wood for cooking and heating. He says the first day of school the teacher called the role and kept saying, "Diamond Hedrick, Diamond Hedrick, Isn't your name Diamond Hedrick?" He told her no. She asked his name. "Get Wood," he replied. This has always been Diamond's favorite joke. He was the wood gatherer for his family, because he was the only one to get it to suit his daddy.

These were lean years and all toys the children had, they had to invent themselves. Back then, the children had such imaginations. From early age, Diamond always thought about what he wanted to do when he grew up. He wanted to be a logger, building roads, driving big trucks, and working in construction. Delmas Lewis drove a big logging truck by Diamond's house every day, and he wanted to be just like him. When he made his toys he made his dream jobs. Mary was thrifty and she saved everything to make their toys with. Her cream cans were used to make the many trucks Diamond needed in his construction jobs. He used nails to make axels and a six inch board would make the frame. He took a small can to make the hood and a larger can to make the cab. The wheels he would make were out of slices of branches. Then he made little dozers from the many spools Mary saved from her sewing projects. He would take all of this over on the big dirt bank over on the hillside, where he did all of his construction jobs.

There were many happy days he and his brother Loyd, nephew Harvey, and cousins Vance and Jimtom, played together on the hillside. They had to learn to share, because cream cans were scarce. Mary only used cans of cream when she was baking cakes. That was the only thing Diamond was allowed to bum. He told everyone to save their cans for him. He made trucks and dozers for the boys when they brought him cans and spools. These boys were always spending nights with each other. The funniest story is how Diamond had to tie Jimtom to the bed post at night, because he sleep-walked. One night they found him in the loft out on the rafters and that was to scary, so Diamond took his belt and strapped him to the bed post from then on.

One day, Diamond and Vance decided to dig a cave so they didn't have to go home when it rained. They decided to go home and pack a lunch, then meet back to eat together. Mary made Diamond a lunch of streaked meat and biscuit and he hurried back to the spot they were supposed to meet. Vance was nowhere around and after a while Diamond went to find him. He found Vance up in a tree with Mary's cow underneath. He was so mad he said, "That cow ate my lunch!" Diamond shared his lunch with his cousin that day.

Diamond remembers how he would borrow his Dad's hammer and kept misplacing it. One day he said, "Come with me, Son. I'll make you a hammer, then you leave mine alone." Diamond helped his dad in the blacksmith shop turning the blower.

The first thing he, Loyd, and their cousin Jimtom built with that new hammer was a small log cabin on Band Land. His dad really worried about that, because Band Land is Indian property, which pretty much surrounded their land. Not to cause trouble, they moved it on down the hill on their property. Diamond eventually lost his newly made hammer and his dad would be plowing thirty years later, when he plowed it up. He would take it to Diamond on that day.

Old home place with milking scene

CHAPTER TWO

Christmas Wagon

One Christmas, Diamond and Loyd got a little red Christmas wagon. It was something hard for Mary and Jasper to afford back then and it had a purpose to be used for. It was to be used by Diamond to get in the fire wood for heating and for cooking. It was a beautiful red Western Flyer and not to be used like one he had built, that he called his guiding wagon. The guiding wagon was built out of twelve inch boards and the axles and wheels were made out of black gum, which is very strong. He was always taking it over on the hillside.

Diamond had devised a steering system and also made a seat for it. He had many years of fun riding it down the steep hillside. When Santa Clause brought them the new red wagon, Jasper told them not to take it where they took the guiding wagon. It simply wasn't strong enough and that would tear it up.

Diamond couldn't stand it and had to do it on the first day. One time down that hill bent everything and the axle folded completely back under the bottom. Diamond dreaded telling his dad that he had done exactly what he told him not to do. Jasper was sitting in the house with Mary, when Diamond had to face him with the bad news. Jasper asked, "Son, where is it at?" Diamond told him it was outside. Mary and Jasper went out to look at the wagon they had to sacrifice so much to buy. Mary asked, "Jap, you can fix it can't you?" Jap is what everyone called Jasper.

Diamond was scared, but he could see his dad grinning a little bit and that told him everything was going to be alright. Jasper said, "You had to do it, didn't you, Son?" He told Diamond if he would help him in the blacksmith shop turning the blowers he would fix it. Jasper had it fixed better than new in about two hours and Diamond never took it down the hill again.

CHAPTER THREE

The Loving Fields

Mary would somedays wake the sleeping children in early morning and head out to where the wild strawberries grew. Roma was a small child of three years old when they would walk a long way into what is called, "the Lovin Fields." They were fields that were owned by Grade and Fannie Lovin.

This was the most special place, where strawberries were so plentiful they could pick all they could carry home. Roma had to be carried some of the way and the small little girl would eat as many as she picked. Every now and then she would have a few more to show her mommy and Mary would always brag on how good she did each time she showed her small amount. Mary would catch her looking away and slip a few more into her basket to make her feel good. They all ate the berries as well and still brought home a bountiful harvest. Mary was one of the fastest berry pickers and her children will all admit this. One could only imagine the preserves, cakes, and pies the berries would make when they got them home.

The children and Mary had to work so hard in the spring and summer months. After they spent the morning in the field they would all walk back to the house, where Mary would cook their dinner. Just as soon as their dinner settled they went back to the fields. Mary would have to milk again to finish off the day with another two gallons of milk. She would make a lot of butter and buttermilk with that milk. Mary never drank milk at all, but Jasper loved buttermilk with cornbread. The rest of the family loved to drink lots of milk and eat cornbread and milk, which is called a "milk mess." On Big Snowbird, they have what is called a "coffee mess." You first crumble up biscuits with butter, then drench the biscuits with coffee and cover this with gravy. Mary always made all of these for Diamond, her special pet.

Old home place with milking scene

One morning, they were all working in the corn field when Mary left and walked back to the house. The older girls went with her and Diamond, Loyd, and Roma were told to stay in the field. The boys were told to keep on working and three year old Roma was told to stay with Diamond. Minnie Jo walked down the trail to Marvin and Gladys's house to fetch Gladys. Later that evening, they were told their mommy had gave birth to a baby that was stillborn. Mary and Jasper would have had nine children instead of seven, but they lost the first and the last babies at birth.

All the babies were spaced out with the breastfeeding that controlled the births. Diamond's joke was that he was such a hard baby to wean off the breast and that his mommy had to put black stuff on her breast to wean him. He said it didn't work, he just licked it off and cried for more. This is not a joke, like so many of Diamonds funny stories, this really is a true story! After the garden came in, the hardest work for the family started. This was back before electricity had come to Snowbird. Not having any electricity meant no refrigerators or freezers, so the only preserving was canning or drying. All the preserving of berries and apples didn't let up until everything that could possibly be put away to eat was preserved for the winter months. Jasper grew and dried his own pinto beans for the winter time. He grew sweet potatoes and they were wrapped in paper and stored in the loft of the house.

Jasper had the most beautiful apple orchard. He grew Macintosh, Whopper jaw, Cortland, Green Pippin, Red and Golden Delicious, and Winesap. The ones that came in first were the Red and Yellow June apples that ripened in June and were very good. One Apple Jasper found growing in the woods he would burry in the ground and dig up at Christmas time. Jasper never knew the name of this apple.

The children would cut up apples into thin slices and Mary would put them on a clean sheet up on the roof to dry. This was dried fruit for stack cakes and cooked fruit for fried pies and biscuits. This was such delicious eating. Diamond would say, "We lived like kings."

Apple Orchard

Kraut making was a very tedious thing to accomplish. There are so many rules that you had to follow. If a girl had her period, she didn't make kraut at that time. It supposedly would ruin it, making it turn black. Also, when the signs were in the bowels and in the knees, you couldn't make kraut. One fall when the cabbage heads got big enough and it was krauting time, Mary suddenly had a gallbladder attack and had to go to the hospital. Minnie Jo, who was the oldest girl at home, had to make the kraut. Jasper had a new hammer and he told Minnie Jo to use it to pack the kraut down tight into the quart jars. After Minnie washed the hammer's handle real good, she tapped and packed it good and tight. Minnie Jo always tried to please her dad, so she packed it good! She carried the jars of kraut to the meat house and after carefully putting them down she shut the door. Just as the door closed, she heard the biggest explosions going off. She tried to open the door, but couldn't. Kraut was going everywhere, all over the precious meat. Hams, shoulders, and midlands were all covered in the kraut. When Jasper finally let Minnie Jo go back in, she had the biggest mess to clean up.

All summer there was something for the kids to do. Stringing beans was a real important job for the kids to help with. This was all for the many cans of beans and leather britches. Jasper's favorite was pickled beans and corn. Diamond did not like them and would not eat them. Jasper always tried to make him to eat them until Mary intervened, telling him he might as well leave him alone.

The corn field was where a lot of work and planning were important. This was carefully thought out year after year. Jasper would plant corn, beans, and pumpkins together. It made a lot of sense, because the corn stalk held up the bean vines that came in first. He raised pumpkins in the same field, so when he cut the corn tops and pulled the fodder he would create a tee pee with the tops that would protect the pumpkins from the frost bite. The boys would pull all the corn leaves (fodder) and bundle it together and tie it on the corn stalk to cure out to make feed for the horse and cows. He could raise more beans, pumpkins, and corn than anyone.

Nothing was ever wasted. After the corn was all gathered and the fodder was in the barn, the last thing was to make the fertilizer for the next year. Jasper made a tool that the boys used to go through the field, cutting the remaining corn stalks into little pieces to mix back into the soil. Jasper also had the wife and children that were always eager to please him and they were not afraid of back breaking work. Nobody could hoe as fast as Mary. She would hoe her row and meet Diamond half way up his.

When the corn was ready to be ground into meal, it was Diamond's job to take it to the mill. Jasper was very particular about how it was ground and Diamond knew exactly how fine he liked it. Jasper was bullish about his cornmeal. He believed his cornmeal made the best cornbread. When Three Rivers cornmeal came out in the grocery store, everyone was singing the praises about what good cornbread it made. One night, Jasper was bragging what good cornbread Mary had made, as he usually did. This night he went on and on, then he saw a little smile come across Mary's mouth and he said, "Mary, you didn't!"

A funny story was the preacher, Ronald Holland, was talking with some men that worked with him for the state. They were bragging on their big potatoes. Ronald thought of Jasper's, so he made a bet. He said, "Let's all bring our biggest taters tomorrow and we'll see who has the biggest one." Ronald went straight to Jasper's that evening and Jasper took him out to his tater bin. Ronald said he had never seen such a pretty bunch of potatoes in all his life. He picked out the biggest one and Jasper let him have it. Ronald won that bet!

Along with all the preserving came fixing the grapes, tomatoes, okra, and beets. Diamond had the extra job of shelling corn for hominy. He had to find the biggest grains for his mommy to make it with. She would mix ashes and red devil lye together, pour it over the corn to get the husk off, and then wash it very good.

Pumpkins were a really good food that everybody loved. Not just for pies, but cooked pumpkin made into a butter that they slathered on biscuits. "Pumpkin messes" were biscuits crumbled with butter, drenched in coffee, then the pumpkin butter slathered on top of that. Mary made a lot of delicious things with pumpkin. Diamond recalls when he had to cut up pumpkin to feed to the cow and how the cow could make you so hungry watching her eat it. This would be fed to the cow while she was being milked. She ate the hull and all.

Some days, Mary would give the kids a biscuit and let them go out to the tomato patch to eat lunch. Diamond would say, "That was good a site!" Mary had a saying you could set your clock by. If the sun was shining and a sudden shower of rain came up, at the same time the next day you would have another shower. Another rule the children couldn't break was if the leaves were showing their underside, they could not go swimming in the creek. This was because she knew a storm might be coming and the creek could swell and wash them away.

During the dog days of summer, the children often had sores on their bodies. This was due to a form of infection known as "Impetigo." This wasn't abnormal, since the children spent hours outdoors in the elements. Mary was tasked with doctoring the many sores made worse by swimming in the creeks and lakes. Even though his Mommy told him not to go swimming in the creek, Diamond says they would sneak and go in anyway. He remembers he got his hinny busted many times for disobeying his mommy.

CHAPTER FOUR

Ted's blood

When Diamond was a small boy, he was always sickly. He had a lot of skin infections with blister like boils all over his body. Mary had a treatment to draw the poison out of a boil. She would take a piece of salty fat back pork and wrap it on the boil. The next morning the boil would come to a head, so it could be squeezed out and heal. He stayed sick with colds and pneumonia a lot of the time and his young life was pretty miserable. When he was eleven years old the doctor took his tonsils out. This surgery would almost cost him his life.

The truth was, Diamond hadn't been the baby for a while. Loyd, his little brother who followed him everywhere and idolized him, had taken his place with mommy. Diamond really resented how he just climbed up in her lap, even when he needed her. Even when it came to getting his tonsils out, he had to share that with Loyd, too. What could have been some extra Pettin' had to be shared with Loyd. When they got to the hospital, the six year old Loyd was scared of everything. Diamond figured he might as well be the stronger one, which he would be appreciated for.

After they both had their tonsils out everything went good, but the next morning Loyd slipped out of the room by himself to try to go home. He got up and out the door before they knew it. After they found him out in the parking lot they brought him in. Dr. Van Gorder had a talk with him and Diamond. He told them both that they better not be crying, because if they did all this will break loose and have to be done all over again. After going home, Loyd cried the whole time, night and day. Diamond was old enough to realize how bad it really would be to have to go through all of that again. He made up his mind he was not going to cry, not ever.

He was on the porch and saw the one person he loved more than anything coming down the trail to see him. Grandpa Pose was a very loving grandparent. He was everything to the family, including the button keeper. After talking to Mary and Diamond for a few minutes, Mary asked Grandpa if he had a button she needed.

Grandpa reached into his pocket and pulled out his collection of buttons. After Mary found the one she needed, she went back into the house to sew it on.

Diamond was resting with his one elbow on grandpa's knee and looking up at his timeless face. Grandpa had his hand around the still very sick grandson and he was telling a story about the pet crow he and Grandma had. Grandma had been missing her shinny things and what-nots. Coins went missing until Grandpa was out in the wood shed and saw the crow bring some more of Grandma's trinkets and stash them in a box in the top of the shed. In the box were all of Freddie's things she had been missing.

It was a wonderful day until the blood started pouring from Diamonds nose and mouth. Grandpa hollered, "Mary, Diamond's bleeding to death!" They didn't have a car back then, but Novella lived just up the road. Her husband, Judd Hyde, had one and he was immediately ready to go. The family all jumped in the car and headed out to the Andrews Hospital.

The day had gone into night by the time they got to the old gravel road around the Topton curves. There were no street lights back then and treacherous, narrow, winding curves that dropped off a long way down. The headlights paled against the dark foggy night. They were lucky to have a flash light and it was also good that Diamond's brother, Ted, went along as well. Ted sat on the fender of the car around the dark curves holding a flash light for Judd to see his way.

Diamond nearly bled to death that night and Mary had to pull the bloody clots out of Diamonds throat to keep him from choking to death. He was unconscious when they got there. Dr. Charles VanGorder told them if this boy didn't get some blood in thirty minutes he was going to die. Again, they would find out how good it was to have Ted come along. It just so happened Ted had the blood match they needed to save him. Dr. Van Gorder laid him down beside Diamond, where he saved his brother's life. Diamond was unconscious for six days and when he came out of it, he was so hungry. Jasper had gone out to get lunch and had brought a hamburger back for Mary. Hungry little Diamond wanted it so bad. Mary told Jasper to take that out of there, because she was not eating until her baby could eat.

When Dr. Van Gorder came back into the room, he started to remove the packing from Diamond's nose. He told him he was going to want to sneeze worse than ever in his life and if he did, it would all have to be done all over again! It was hard, but Diamond made it through without sneezing. They brought a first meal of chicken broth and it was mighty good. Life soon got back to normal and everyone got back on track. When Diamond got in trouble with his parents, he would always blame it on Ted's ole bad blood. That's what was making him do the mean things and he couldn't help it!

The Rolling Store

CHAPTER FIVE

Day of the Rolling Store

There was one day a week that the children, as well as adults, looked forward to. On Thursdays, Laura Phillip's rolling store came to Big Snowbird. Diamond and his siblings, Loyd and Roma, along with his uncle Marvin's children, Jimtom, Pat, and Judy would join up with another uncle John's children, Joy, Geraldine, and Arbara Jean to spend the money they worked out on whatever their hearts desired. All these cousins were close in age, as well as close in life.

Jack Odom, who drove the rolling store, was always joking and liked all the little kids. He was always patient and willing to trade for almost anything. Jasper always made sure the kids had eggs to trade and when a hen would stop laying he would tie her legs together and give her to Diamond to trade her for what they wanted. Jack would put the hen in a box underneath the truck.

The deal Jasper made with Diamond was if he fed and watered the chickens and gathered the eggs for the week, he would give him six eggs to trade. Jack was a good man and he was more than fair with the children. He always made sure they got what they wanted.

The kids would go with Mary to pick blackberries. She would let them sell them at the top of Dobson Hill on rolling store day. If they didn't sell them, Jack would usually trade for them. All the kids wanted candy, but Diamond always wanted bologna. Loyd and Jimtom would eat their candy, then want some of Diamond's bologna. Now, Diamond was selfish with his precious bologna. There was only one person he would share that with, his little sister, Roma.

One day while they were all waiting for the store to come, a man with a nice car pulled over with a flat tire very close to where they were waiting. He asked Diamond, Jimtom, and Loyd, if they would change the flat for him. He told them he would pay them a dollar a piece. They really enjoyed the rolling store that day. It turns out the man owned Fallstaff Beer and his name was Ed Brookman. He would later build Brookman Lodge, which later became Blue Boar Lodge. Jimtom always joked about planting that tack in the road.

Another night during the week was Friday night. That night, all the families went to Uncle John's. John had one of the first televisions in the area. Most all the Hedricks' and their children visited that night to watch boxing. Jasper is said to have been a pretty good boxer himself. All the cousins were so close and enjoyed getting together. None of the women cared much for boxing, so they would hang out in the kitchen. When it was warm they would sit out on the porch. All the children would run wild! Grandma Freddie really enjoyed getting to be with her grandchildren and great grandchildren, she didn't like the boxing either. The Hedrick men all loved that special night.

Jasper's sister, Nitter, and husband, Ed, would come and the joke he told was she only came so she wouldn't have to kiss him goodbye. Ed and Nitter were blessed with twin girls, Ollie and Dollie. Another one of the Hedrick's jokes was when Nitter was giving birth, Ed was plowing the field. A man came down and told him, "Ed, you got a girl." Ed just kept on plowing. After a little while the man came back, "You got another girl." Ed says to horse, "Whoah! I got to get up there and put a stop to this!"

Ed and Nitter Stewart were a very happy couple. Most people referred to Nitter as Netter-Ed. Ollie and Dollie were about one year older than Diamond. These two little girls were absolutely beautiful. The Hedricks are really good looking people. They also raised a son who was born to John Hedrick's daughter, Barbara Ann. They loved and raised him as their own. They named him Nathan and along with his twin sisters they had a beautiful family.

CHAPTER SIX

Baptizing Jimtom

Diamond was a young budding preacher man. When someone's little pet would die all the cousins would all get together and Diamond would preach its funeral. They would gather in the wood yard and when he would get through, they would bury it beside the chicken pen under the holly tree. Diamond would always take it upon himself to try to save their littles souls. He would remind them at Arabra Jean's little cat's funeral that he knew Kitty had lived a good life. He knew she went to heaven and if they wanted to ever see little Kitty again, they had to make it right and be ready to go. Looking out at Jimtom he told him, "Jimtom, you just might as well come on down, the Lord's dealing with you." Jimtom came on down.

Diamond Preaching

Next Sunday, Diamond baptized Jimtom at the "Big Hole." All the cousins were there and they walked down to the Big Hole. Finding a seat on the big beautiful rock, they were all so happy. Diamond and Jimtom waded out into the middle of the creek in waist deep water. Diamond put one hand behind Jimtom's head, held the other hand to Heaven, and repeated the words he heard so many times from his Uncles who preached. "Dear Father who art in Heaven, I baptize my brother in the name of the Father, the Son, and the Holy Ghost." He held Jimtom under and was making sure he was completely baptizing him. Everyone was crying and wailing, because Diamond was holding him under too long! Diamond said he wanted to be sure all his sins got washed away.

The weekends were special, too. Saturday, Mary took Lennox and Loyd with her to the chicken lot, where she picked out three fryers. They took their .22's and they were crack shots. They would also help their mother pluck their feathers and clean them up. Mary would cut them up and have them ready for Sunday morning to go into two big black iron skillets. She would fry all of that fresh chicken and make gravy over it. GOOD! Now that was Sunday breakfast, but if the preacher came she would have it for dinner instead. Sometimes she would just cook more chicken.

No matter who came, Mary's children were always served first. She would seat her children on the end of the porch and bring their plates to them, making sure they had their favorite parts. Mary always had a little dog and Diamond remembers how she would make it's little plate of food just like theirs. He says it would eat as good as they did. She loved her family and she loved her little squirrel dog.

CHAPTER SEVEN

Polio Comes Knocking

After the morning service at Cedar Cliff and the Sunday meal was over, the Hedrick's would go to Mt. Nebo Church about two o'clock for another service. The children would all get together Sunday evening and play ball. Mary Hedrick made the best soft balls out of old socks. She rolled them so tightly and they never came undone. She also made dolls for Roma and the other little girls. The children played fox and dog (hound), hop scotch, hide and seek, tag you're it, guess what I'm doing, and red rover.

There were eight or more children, pretty much all cousins, that would gather up on what they called "the top." There were Marvin and Glady's kids: Pat, Jimtom, Judy, Buster, and Gerald. Then there was John and Maggie's kids: Barbara Ann, Van, Joy, Geraldine, Arbara Jean, and Randall. Their oldest daughter, Barbara Ann, who was older and said to be one of the most beautiful girls to come out of these hills, didn't hang out with the younger ones. Diamond remembers her beauty and her sweet beautiful southern voice. All John's girls were very beautiful girls.

Polio Comes Knocking

Carol Collins and little brother William

19

John and Maggie's Daughter Arbara Jean was stricken with Polio when the epidemic hit the United States. Carol Collins and Neil Patterson of Robbinsville were also stricken. Carol was only eighteen months old. Diamond remembers the day before Arbara got sick. They had the best time playing all over the top of Dobson Hill. They all played so hard and Arbara was so alive and feeling great. The next morning Diamond and the cousins showed up on the top to play, where they were met by Arbara's sisters, Joy and Geraldine. They told how she got sick that night and had to go the doctor. That evening everyone knew Arbara had Polio and she would have to spend many months in an iron lung. She had Bulbar Polio. She was paralyzed from the neck down. A surgery she had on her hands gave her back some use of her arms and hands, but she would never walk again.

She went on to finish school with her younger sister, Geraldine. Diamond loved his little cousin Arbara as he loved all his cousins, they were all very good playmates. He was so pleased he could carry his little cousin in his arms on and off the bus in the mornings and on and off in the evenings. Doyle Hyde helped to carry her wheel chair. The cousins would have to play on the top without Arbara from then on. Diamond has always remembered that last day he played with Arbara. Diamond was close with all his cousins in this big Hedrick clan, but he was always closer to his girl cousin, Joy, than any.

They would sometimes play in the meadow and on one day they were flipping rocks over to see what they could see. There were all kinds of monsters under those rocks for the curious kids to find. On this day they found a black snake with two heads. They almost had it killed when their dads came along and stopped them. Jasper and John took it to the school laboratory. Diamond believes it wound up in Cherokee.

Leslie and Annie's kids that were young enough to be in the games on the top were Vance, Chad, Leonard, Edna, and Nellie. They also had Christine, Vernon, and Ruth that were all older. They also had a young son, Chucky, who died at around a year old. Diamond's cousin Vance was closest to his age and they played together a lot. They also sold a paper called "Grit." They walked and rolled a wheel barrow to hold the papers. When it didn't make them enough money to leave their very important chores, it didn't last for long.

Glen and Nettie's kids were Doyle, Loretta, Barry, Mary Anne, Gail, and Katherine. These were some more cousins that were all close. If they had squabbles they weren't many and didn't last long. When they got play time they didn't waste it on fighting. All the kids had to work hard helping their families survive.

The children had to make their own entertainment. Over on the hillside were many leaves and pine needles to make their sliding boards. Minnie Jo prided herself in having the best one. In the fall, they had the broom sage that made even better sliding boards.

This was a time when things were rationed, because of World War ll. It was the things like sugar, salt, flour, and coffee. To make sure they got everything that was needed for their families they sent older sister Minnie Jo and her cousin Barbara Ann, who was the same age as she was, to their Great Uncle Will's store. They got there as soon as the ration truck, so they didn't miss out on getting the supplies. The two girls had a long journey across the mountain, usually taking all day. The girls would always have candy bar money and mostly bought Baby Ruths. They always made it back to a big stump on the mountain top that was half way home before they ate their candy bars.

All the children on Snowbird went barefoot in the spring and summer months. Diamond remembers when he got his Brogans. His dad would go out and cut sticks for the ones that needed shoes. He would measure their feet with the sticks and then cut the sticks off. He then put the sticks in his pocket. Mary went with him to the store and she would pick out the girls' and he picked out the boys'. Diamond says they always felt good and he never complained. The first frost they wore their new shoes with pride.

Flour and feed came in sacks that were in the most beautiful colors and prints. The mothers were able to fashion the most beautiful shirts and dresses for their families out of these. Back then Diamond remembers the most handsome shirts that they handed down from one brother to another.

Roma loved her dresses her mommy fashioned for her with her special knack. All their clothes were ironed beautifully and Diamond remembered the many patches he had to wear that his mother sewed into his britches and overalls. Most of all they went to school with clean clothes. Diamond hated wash day, having to carry many loads of wood to heat the wash pot, then to heat the stove for ironing.

One day at school, a very hateful teacher criticized the patches on his britches, telling him not to come back to school until he had better clothes. She took the hand of the scared little boy and whacked it with a ruler. Diamond was held back, because he was afraid to go to school anyway and this made him afraid to go back the next day. When he showed his mommy the welt she left on his hand and told her he didn't want to go back, she was furious! She said, "You are going back and I am going with you." Mary couldn't wait to get there the next morning. She hurried in her little fast steps and found herself face to face with a very surprised teacher. Mary asked why she had made fun of his clothes and made him so frightened to go back to school. With that she grabbed her and gave her what is to be called a "good whooping!" Diamond thinks that teacher might have left town, because he never saw her again. Nobody messed with Jasper and Mary's kids.

Roma was always the perfect little sister. She always kept her big brother's shoes polished and shined. She would iron his britches and put creases in them in the same way her older sister Minnie Jo had done for her. There was always a close bond to the Hedrick brothers and sisters and there will be until the "rapture" gets them. That's a religious term they use a lot. That's when God comes back and takes the saved people and leaves the wicked. Whoa be the woman with the suckling baby that's not ready to go. Two people will be working in the field and all of a sudden one will be gone (the rapture took them.)

Ice cream was a treat they hardly ever had. One day the Deacons of the church got together and paid the ice cream truck to bring out all the ice cream the children could eat. Diamond and Vance tried to out eat each other and nearly got foundered that day. It was a long time before they could eat ice cream again. Chocolate Rogers drove the Coble ice cream truck that day. All the adults enjoyed watching those children eat ice cream.

The Hedrick's didn't have electricity until Diamond was twelve years old. It simply hadn't come to Big Snowbird yet. When it came, they were all so excited having lights. Especially Diamond, who had to figure out what made that light bulb burn. By sticking his finger in the socket, he found out firsthand!

Before they got refrigeration they would borrow ice from Marvin and Gladys'. Roma loved going to get that refreshing ice. She remembers how good that ice looked. It made Kool Aid taste better and the refreshing birch drink Mary always made out of birch bark. If she didn't have bark, she would make it with boiling little twigs. She would serve it in glasses that came out of a box of oatmeal, or from snuff. Mary didn't want her children to know she dipped, so she was always discreet. She had a little black gum stick that made the best little snuff brush. Mary enjoyed her dip of snuff. Gramma Freddie loved hers, too. She didn't hide hers, being older it was more excepted. She put hers on their bee stings and insect bites. It went on poison oak and poison ivy rashes, too.

CHAPTER EIGHT

Mary, Where's My Tooth Pullers?

Diamond's household was pretty normal, except when some poor person suffering from a tooth ache showed up at their door looking for Jasper. He had a set of tooth pullers he practiced dentistry with. Lots of people brought their children to get their teeth pulled, so you would hear a lot of screaming from time to time. Diamond would run like a turkey! It was a whole lot like hog killing times, which made him run too. He couldn't stand animals being killed or teeth getting pulled. He always left hog killing to his dad and his brothers.

Then one day, Jasper couldn't find his tooth pullers. Arvil Waldroup had come to get a tooth pulled. Jasper asked Mary where his pullers were. Mary told him she would never tell him, because she could no longer stand to hear people screaming. She never told him where she hid them. That secret went with her to her grave.

Mary was like a doctor on call, so one day Diamond was watching Jasper show horses. He was watching so intently when he stepped back into his dad's big drawing knife, splitting his heel wide open. He didn't make a sound, he would no way let his dad know he had been so careless. Only one thing to do, run to Mommy! When Jasper realized there had to be an accident with all the blood on the ground he ran to the house, where he found his very skilled wife putting Diamond's heel back together.

Diamond was sharpening a very sharp mowing blade when his pointer finger slipped nearly cutting it off. Mary put coal oil on it, then put it back together. She bandaged it up as good as a doctor could and it healed completely. Almost all the feeling came back. Diamond always would say his mommy's lap was the best healing place and the best place to take the pain away.

Mary would always say she knew what it felt like to lose a yougun', because when Ted was seven years old he had pneumonia fever. Mary had doctored and doctored, doing everything she knew to do. When he hadn't improved and got so much worse, she called in Dr. Spade. He came out to the house and after examining the lifeless Ted, pronounced him dead. Coming out of the room, he gave Mary the awful news. Mary was inconsolable and in disbelief. She went into an uncontrollable screaming and crying fit. Pose and Freddie drug her out to the barn, where she wouldn't be seeing Ted. They held onto her so tightly, trying without much success to comfort her.

Jasper's brother, Marvin and Harley Conseen, an Indian friend, came by the barn and Grandpa told them Ted had died. They went over to the house and Harley, with the help of Marvin, started working and rubbing on Ted, trying to push the life back into the lifeless boy.

Harley loved all the Hedrick's, but Ted was his favorite little helper in the blacksmith shop. Ted would turn the blowers for Harley and they had become real good friends, even though Harley was thirty some years older than Ted. Anytime any of the Hedrick children were sick, Harley and his brother, Joby, would set up at night with them. Harley seeing the life gone out of Ted felt that this was not acceptable. After they started moving his arms and legs they did finally push the life back into his lifeless body. All this until Ted started breathing again.

He was then taken to Fort Sanders Hospital in Knoxville Tennessee, where Dr. Alexander took care of him. He was there fourteen days. Grandma Hedrick stayed with him the whole time until he was able to return home.

Jasper was always a visionary and he was always preparing for the winter months, getting enough food to feed his family. Everyone says he could never enjoy life in the beautiful summer months for worrying about what was coming. He also worried about his brother's and sister's families. He was the leader of the family. It wasn't just for his own use that he always kept a horse. He would loan him out with the plow inside the sled. Even if Jasper needed his horse that day, he would loan him anyway. He gave everyone strict instructions on taking care of his horse. He told them treat him good, let him take his time, and be sure to feed him at dinner time. With that, he put 6 ears of corn into a sack and tied it to the Haimes and told them to just let him eat out of the back of the sled.

Dan was a horse that Diamond loved so much. He didn't need any check lines, he knew more about the job than they did. Jasper always said, "Now boys, just hold the plow and Dan will do the rest." Diamond would get so sorry for Dan and at the end of the row he would go pet him. Diamond says if there is a horse Heaven, he's sure Dan's there.

CHAPTER NINE

Snowbird Loses A Giant

Diamond always wanted to be strong and smart like his dad. He always wanted to be able to flip the turning plow like Jasper did, he had always let the horse turn it. Finding out too late, that wasn't as fun as he thought it would be. Jasper was a jack of all trades and he was one of the best blacksmiths around. This was something he learned from his father, Posey Hedrick.

Pose, as they called him, was a gentle giant and a lot of people said he was the stoutest man they knew. Pose loved the little birds and when he would go out on his porch and sit down, Freddie would bring bread crumbs and put them in his pocket. All of a sudden, all the little birds would come and dip down into the pocket, helping themselves to easy pickings. Then they would gather in his beautiful white hair and scratch his scalp. Frieda was her name, but everyone called her Freddie. Pose's passion in life was taking care of his little wife, Freddie. He did everything her heart desired to keep her happy.

As a young man, Pose was crippled when he had typhoid fever, but he never let anything stop him from doing what had to be done. He had made himself two walking canes and every morning he would get up and wrap his legs in bandages to keep them from swelling. Pose was very upset when he was crippled, but he was one to rise above. He invented many things to help out in his life. One thing was called a lazy gal. He took a wheel off of a model tee and made a pulley with rope and wire. This he hooked to a bucket that went across a post down the hill to the spring. This brought their water back up to the house.

The only time Diamond could remember Grandpa Hedrick getting mad at him and his cousin Vance, was when they bent his bucket. They were turning it loose to run down the hill to see how fast it would go. He told them he better never see them do that again, that was not to play with.

The problem of carrying in wood he solved too. He made him a box with two straps, one on each side. He would load the box with wood, sit down on a block, and back into it. When he wanted to unload it, he would sit on the edge of the porch, and lay back sliding his arms out.

Grandpa Posey Hedricks Homeplace

He was also a really good craftsman, he loved making things for everyone. He had his workshop in an old school bus. His tools were very old-timey. He had a drawing knife and a lot of crude tools like a hand grinder to sharpen things with. He had made a seat that he could sit facing the large grinding wheel, so he could turn it with his feet. He also had a water drip that kept the grinder from over- heating. He always kept glass to smooth the handles for hammers, grab skips, hoes, knives, peavies, and most all tools that he made handles for.

Loyd recalls Grandpa taking down a groundhog hide and with his very sharp knife cutting the straightest straps for shoestrings for his shoes. He was always drying a hide of some kind. He would stretch them on a board and put talcum on them until they were stiff and dry enough to cut things out of.

The children loved the toys he made. If he made one something, he made all of them something. He made popguns, whirligigs, and the best sling shots. Diamond loved the slingshots the best. He loved crafting chairs, tables, beds, and everything they needed, he provided.

Grandma Freddie was treated like a queen. Grandpa always made sure she got her nap. If the children came over in the evening when Grandma was sleeping, her loyal bodyguard Pose would make sure they didn't wake her up. He adored her.

Grandpa Pose and Grandma Freida Hedrick

One of the saddest days Diamond can remember was the day his Grandpa died. Arvil Adams had come over in the evening when Pose was putting up his chickens. Arvil would sometimes drop by to bring him tools he needed fixed. Pose told him to go on into the house and he would be right in. With this he was hurrying and got really short of breath. When he set down in his chair he fell over, tipping the chair over. He landed in the doorway in between the kitchen and the living room. He had expired.

Diamond was just up the road with his cousins JC and Junior, when his Uncle John drove up in his little red Jeep. He told Diamond, "Dad's dead. Go tell your dad and Marvin, and I'll tell Leslie, Niter, and Nettie." Diamond's friends told him when he got back they would go with him to his Grandpa's house.

When the whole family had gathered around, they appointed Jasper to go through his pockets. That was the saddest thing Jasper ever had to do at that point in his life. This man was always a fixer, so in his pockets he had yards of string, nuts, bolts, screws, and oh yes, buttons! Every time Jasper would pull something out of a pocket he would break down and say, "Now Dad, what were you going to do with this?" Then Jasper's brothers helped him remove his shoes and unwrap the bandages he had wrapped his legs in that morning. The funeral director, Charles Pearson, came and he and another man took Pose to the funeral parlor. This was a very hard time for everyone. They all stayed at the house with the very frail Grandma.

Everyone had their stories about this amazing father and grandpa, but one story always stood out for Diamond. Jasper tells how he and his brothers were fishing with their dad, when the biggest diamondback rattlesnake leaped hitting him and knocked him to the ground, swiftly biting him above his ankle. Jasper rolled on the ground with him until he got the huge fangs out of his leg. Pose did what most people did for a snake bite, cutting across the bite mark and sucking out the poison.

They carried the sick boy home, where he would find some moonshine and pour down his son's throat. In most of the homes back then, it was kept for medical purposes as well as whoop-ty-do! Pose's was for medical only. Pose rounded up a whole case of dynamite and blew that rock pile to kingdom come. Pose loved his children and he could never let that snake get by with that!

All of Jasper's life he would be reminded on the anniversary, because he would get sick and a red streak would run up his leg. He could never have honey bees, because a sting would nearly kill him, but his father had sure taught that snake a thing or two.

These stories went on all night and never anything but good about Pose. All night the poor little grandma kept saying, "What am I going to do without Pose?" Everybody wondered the same, because they knew she really depended on him. It wasn't just that, she really did love him. He was her soulmate and the most pleasant human being she could ever share her life with. Even when she didn't get her way, which was not much, she could pout at Pose and he would always try to make her happy. Pose couldn't stand it when she was unhappy with him.

For three nights, the Indians sang beautiful religious songs. They would stop and drink coffee and then go right back to singing again. Pose's favorite song was, "It's Love." Their group was called The Snowbird Indian Quartet. They were Pose's favorite singers and they loved Pose as everyone did. Pose would sometimes go to their church, which was the Zion Hill Baptist Church. Pose wasn't really affiliated with any certain church, but he would sometimes show up at one usually taking his grandsons. Pose did love the Zion Hill Baptist Church.

The singers could speak English really well, because they had gone to the Indian School. The older Indians could not speak English too good, but they would greet you and say, "Saleo" and "Seiyou" (hello and how are you.) They also told their age was "moon go over many times." Diamond wishes now he had listened harder and learned more about the old Indian ways.

For the next three days, the Indians sang all night. Their soothing voices filled the air all through Sleepy Hollow and all the way up to the top of Dobson Hill. Pose loved all the Indians and they loved him. His spirit was everywhere and everyone that knew him could feel this.

There were so many people at his funeral. It took hours for the viewing and Pose looked so beautiful and peaceful in his coffin after it arrived back home from the funeral home. Pose had made many coffins for other people, but never one for himself. His white hair still gleamed and if you didn't know, you would think Grandpa was napping. He had on his best overalls, the ones he wore to church. His white shirt was starched and ironed to a perfection, just the way Grandma Freddie always kept it.

People brought so much food. There was an assortment of breads, fat back, tators, beans, bean cakes, and chicken. Nothing fancy, just old-timey and very good. The day of the funeral was a beautiful day, but Diamond and everybody woke up with a sad feeling in their heart. By this time the realization had set in, Grandpa was gone.

Grandpa was buried on West Buffalo, where his parents, brothers, and sisters were buried in the Hedrick Cemetery. He and Frieda had three children that died as babies, all buried in the Hedrick cemetery. Roselle Hedrick Aug. 4th, 1913- May 15th, 1915 / Frank Hedrick Dec. 3rd, 1915- Aug. 14th, 1918 / Arthur David Hedrick Oct. 21st, 1918- Oct. 24th, 1918.

It is a beautiful little cemetery off the beaten path. You go up this little road that leads to a small hill top that is as beautiful as lonely when you go there. Such a wonderful family buried there, people that are still being missed!

Benjamin Posey Hedrick, born Nov. 7th, 1886 in Cherokee Co. married Frieda Arizona Long Mar. 6th, 1905. He died Apr. 17th, 1958. Frieda was born on Aug. 12th, 1886. After Pose died, some years later she went on to marry again. She married Lynn Trull after many years of being alone. She died at ninety-eight years old on Jan. 11th, 1984. She is buried beside her loving wonderful husband, Pose.

CHAPTER TEN

Life Without Pose

Freddie was always scared to stay by herself at the house she had shared with Pose. She always had one of her grandchildren stay with her at night. John wanted his mother to be close to him and his family, so she wouldn't be scared. All the sons got together and created the cutest little house out of John's can house. This put her close to John, Maggie, and their children.

One of the grand daughters, Joy's, fondest memories is going to Freddie's house after school and hungrily reaching into the warming cabinet over her little wood cook stove. She was a wonderful cook and always had something delicious for her grand youngun's to eat.

After all the grand kids had grown up and moved away, Grandma really felt the loneliness. Freddie had been alone for several years when she noticed Lynn Trull at her church. He was the music leader and was such a sweet man. He was a musical prodigy and he wrote a lot of great hymnals. He probably knew more about music than anyone around. He often sang with Jasper, practicing every Sunday morning to sing with the choir in church.

Freddie had admired him one day at church and she told one of his granddaughters, Karen Trull, some of her thoughts. Karen said she believed it might be mutual. Freddie said she didn't believe he felt or thought about her at all. Karen made a bet with her that he did. It was after Karen had moved away that things materialized. Soon Freddie would marry Lynn and prove Karen right, he really did love her.

It was hard for Diamond and the family to realize that she could ever love anyone but Pose. With Pose, Freddie had it made and what hurt the grandkids was to see her waiting on a man hand and foot like she never did wait on their Grandpa. Through no fault of his own, they held this against him. The Grandma lived ten very happy years with Lynn until he died.

A funny story about a younger Lynn Trull was how he didn't want to say the word "ass." He was sent to the store by his first wife to purchase Asafetida for his children. He didn't say the ass word, he ask the store clerk for "rump-afetity."

Grandma Hedrick drank yellow root tea every day. Probably one of many reasons she lived to almost one hundred years old. Back then, they had so many good remedies for everything from colds to arthritis. Diamond can never remember Grandma going to the doctor.

Jasper and Mary kept the traditional remedies up. Even rubbing bear grease on their kids feet and putting them toward the stove to help them fight colds. All kinds of poultices were made out of Asafetida and many different concoctions. Diamond said he would have rather been sick than wear it.

Diamond had a stomach burn when he was a young boy. One day, Jasper told him, "Let's go find some Rat Vein and that will stop that." They found it growing right on the ground and it was very hard to find. Jasper broke off a leaf and told Diamond to chew it up and swallow the juice. He says he never tasted anything as bitter in all his life, but it worked. Every time he got the stomach burn, he went back to that place and chewed some more. That's the only place Diamond knew it grew.

A sure remedy for gout was Poke Berries. They would eat the berries and also made juice from them. The best thing for settling your stomach was kraut juice. It was always used by some that had hangovers. The juice of a Touch-me-not was used for sunburns. Moonshine was a good cough medicine and also took the place of alcohol. Diamond would use a little bit as after shave to stop the burn. Red Oak bark was good to boil for toothache. An onion poultice was good for fever. Scraped Irish potatoes were good for a burn.

Mary's brother, Broad, had a relief when you needed to pull your own teeth. You could dig up the root of a smoke vine, dry it, and then smoke it. This would numb the gums. Broad pulled his own teeth that way.

Uncle Leslie and Kit his Mule, and his dog Woodrow

CHAPTER ELEVEN

Uncle Leslie

Jasper's brother, Leslie, was an amazing man. He married Annie Bell Millsaps and had a big family of nine children: Vernon, Christine, Ruth, Nellie, Edna, Vance, Chad, Leonard, and Chucky, who died as a baby.

When Jasper and Leslie were young, they were putting up hay. Jasper threw a pitchfork at a hay stack, hitting Leslie in his left leg. It set up gangrene and had to be amputated. Leslie never let anything hold him back in life. There was another man in Robbinsville that also had one leg, John Howell. They had missing opposite legs, so they shared shoes. John Howell had a shoe repair shop.

Leslie always lived his life to the fullest, always honoring God his whole life. He had a small watch shop in the town of Robbinsville. Every morning he geared up his little donkey, Kit, with just one leg and on crutches. He then drove his buggy six and a half miles into town to work in his watch shop. He fashioned a hoe on the end of a crutch to work his garden. His children worked hard like most all the Hedrick offspring did. The ones that didn't work hard, Jasper referred to as "piss willies." Leslie never let anything get him down. Every day was a beautiful day, it didn't matter if it was over cast or dark. Some days Leslie would hook Kit to the wagon and take Vance and Diamond along the road to pick up the hay the state cut. This was good for winter time to feed the cow and for Kit as well.

Picking up hay

Uncle Leslie hoeing with his crutch with a hoe on the end

When Diamond would spend the night with his cousin Vance, Leslie would get them up early saying, "Get up boys, get up! Annie's got them cat heads on!" Cat heads are what mountain people call biscuits. Leslie would take Diamond and Loyd with two of his boys, Vance and Chad on camping trips. Diamond remembers how Leslie set up their camp with everything they needed and everything was in its place. He would sit in one spot while they ran all over the lake fishing. He caught all the fish and if it wasn't for Leslie, they would have starved for fish.

Uncle Leslie's Camping Trip

Leslie's little mule Kit would get out and all the girls would be so afraid and run back into their houses. They remember when Kit died. They were all sad and a lot of them were at his funeral. So that Kit would fit in the hole in his grave, they had to break his legs. Nobody missed Kit more than Leslie.

Leslie was someone everyone loved to be around, because he was a very good conversationalist. He could come up with really good sermons just by noticing the people in life. Diamond tells about how on the way to church he noticed all the boats heading to the lake. He would say, "This world's gone pleasure mad!" Another sermon was putting on the whole amour of God. If you did this, the Devil couldn't get to you. He would get so happy in church preaching a sermon, he would lean his crutches on the podium and hop around on his one leg.

He also had a good sense for all God's little creatures. Along with his little mule, Kit, he had a little part hound dog, Woodrow, he loved so much. Diamond remembers if they were traveling on the road and a turtle was crossing, he would stop and have Diamond get out to make sure it crossed safely.

A funny story on Leslie was how one day he caught so many fish, way past the limit. He had stuck some in his left trouser leg he always looped over his belt. The Game Warden stopped to talk and Leslie showed him what he had in his fishing creel saying, "I got seven little beauties in here," all the while the fish were jumping in his trouser leg. The Warden said he would never have arrested him, he was also his first cousin.

CHAPTER TWELVE

We're Gonna Keep Him

Jasper was a good conversationalist himself. He loved to talk to everyone after church. His daughters would be wanting to get him going and he was impossible. One day Novella, who was so tired of waiting, asked her mother, "Momma, what are we going to do with Daddy?" Mary replied without a second thought, "We're gonna keep him!"

The Hedricks' all stepped up when they were needed somewhere. If the kids went to a cousin's house at a time they were doing their chores, they knew they could play sooner if they helped their cousins out. A real important time to get together for the families was to raise a barn. Barn raisings were important, because barns were very important structures. Diamond remembers getting to play with all the cousins and friends while the men all pitched in building the much needed barn.

It was a great day for a wonderful picnic that the women would slave over to make for everyone. They would start with fried chicken, fried taters, pinto beans, and always corn bread or biscuits. These times were good memories of families taking pride in being close knit! It's what the world needs now.

Clearing new ground caused them to have many "Ground Clearings," very much like the barn raisings. Life always had things to build and things to do to help people all the time. The churches always looked after people in the community. If somebody needed a new roof or a family lost their home, the church usually stepped in helping rebuild and raising the money needed to rebuild the lives.

A few of the farming families had tobacco allotments. This was hard, profitable work for the whole family. Jasper's was about an acre and you were very fortunate if you got an allotment. It took Jasper a long time to get one. The work started on the last week in February, if the weather was good. Jasper would say, "Boys, we need to get started on that tobacco bed. We've got to get something on it to burn it." They would pile brush and burn every part of the garden, not just the tobacco bed. Next, they would plow the bed up and fertilize it. After sowing the seed, they would cover it with plastic.

When the seedlings got big enough, you pulled them up, and set them out in tobacco rows. You would hoe these plants every week, keeping the weeds chopped out until they got their tops and were around five or six feet tall. You then had to go back through and cut the tops out. From then on, you had to sucker them, breaking the new little sucker that would stunt the plant. Jasper made sure they kept those plants suckered. The plants had to be sprayed once the top was cut to keep the tobacco worm away. The plants were cut once when they turned a beautiful golden yellow. You speared five to a stick and they were hung in the tobacco barn to cure out good and turned a tobacco brown color. They called this "puttin' up backer." When the tobacco cured and came in case, you started grading it. The day had to be a damp day and if the day was hot, the leaves would crack. This meant you got up early and did some every day.

They usually made three grades out of it. To be number one it had to be beautiful golden color, usually the bottom leaves. When you had what they called a hand (about ten leaves,) you would bind them together with a tobacco leaf, wrapping it around the end. You would then have three backer baskets and the 1-2-3 grades of tobacco went into these baskets. There were usually two or three men who drove the tobacco to a warehouse in Knoxville, TN or Asheville, NC. This was real important money for the family. It usually came through about Christmas time.

CHAPTER THIRTEEN

Dr. Van Performs a Miracle

Roma was just a little girl in her mommy's lap at the sewing machine. She stuck her finger under the needle and it went quickly all the way through her finger. Mary was so scared, but she carefully brought that needle back through her little finger. I am so sure she got petting after that! Diamond always says, "Mommy could always pet you back through anything." Roma also had whopping cough when she was little and Mary got her through that, too.

Jasper and JC Duckett were bringing a load of logs out of Santeetlah, when they got half way down the mountain the brakes gave out. JC told Jasper to jump out, because the brakes are gone! They waited as long as they could. The truck was going too fast to jump and having no other way, they both had to jump! Jasper's head hit a big sharp rock that split it open. JC got skinned up all over. The truck kept on going, running off the road, and landing in the top of a big tree. The truck was totaled, but the men would survive that day. Mary put Jasper's head over the sink and washed out the gaping hole. She next shaved the side of his head and wrapped a bandage over the wound. As good as Mary was, there were times when the doctor had to be seen.

Logging has always been a very dangerous job. One day, Jasper was trimming a branch off a log and a smaller tree that was bent by the log suddenly broke loose, jumping up and mashing his Adams Apple to the back of his throat. He was rushed to the clinic in Robbinsville, where Dr. Dick Parett worked his Adams Apple back into place.

Jasper, who always had a beautiful singing voice, could never sing again. He had always been the choir leader, so he made Diamond the leader of the choir. Diamond could always sing better with his dad there beside him. After that, every Sunday Diamond would ask his dad to come up to be beside him. It made him so much braver to have Jasper by his side.

Another accident for Jasper was on the head of Tank Branch. There were ten inches of snow on the ground and he was making a glut (wedge). He was chopping away, when his axe caught an overhead limb and came squarely down on the hand holding the glut. His hand was nearly chopped off and the only thing holding it on was a little skin.

He and Harold Sanook were working for Arvil Adams on this day. Arvil had something else to do, so he dropped them off to work by themselves. They were a long way from civilization, so they walked about five miles to Phil Hollofield's house. They kept the snow packed tightly around the hand. There they would find the State working on the road and they took him to the Parett Clinic, where they tried to do all they could. They knew he needed to go to the Andrews Hospital. There the best surgeon, Dr. Van Gorder, would save his hand.

This happened early one morning and by the time they got to the hospital it would be late in the evening. Dr. Van Gorder took him straight to the operating room, where he connected all the nerves, tissue, and bone. The family waited almost the whole night and finally when Dr. Van Gorder came out, he told them he tried to get everything connected back like it was supposed to be. He said, "We will not know for sure until he gets the cast off if it's going to work right." That was an amazing piece of surgery that night! Dr. Van Gorder was ahead of his time. This family knew that when Jasper's hand completely recovered and he went back to work what a miracle this doctor had performed. Saving Jasper's hand was probably a pretty common surgery for Dr. Van Gorder, but it meant everything to Jasper's family.

Before World War ll, facial reconstruction was not a practiced science. Dr. Van Gorder and Dr. Rodda set up the first field hospital (Mash Unit.) They developed the procedures to save tissue, muscle, bone, and nerve, so when the young men got back home to the United States the surgeons here could re-construct their jaws and all important facial features. These two men did so many miracles on the battle field, saving the lives and limbs of our soldiers that fought in the European Theater.

CHAPTER FOURTEEN

Diamond Saves His Roma!

The Hedrick's' were a fishing family. They all loved to fish and it provided a lot of good food for them. It's probably one reason they have been so healthy. Mary was the fisherman of the family and she could cook them as good as she could catch them. All the adults and younguns' were invited to fish with Mary. She would show up early at their front door and say, "I've got us a lunch packed and I've got us some real nice poles, let's go fishing!" Mary always kept cane poles for fishing.

Diamond remembers walking out Long Hungry Road, going to the lake with his family. Mary would make the most delicious picnics with something for everyone to eat. She made sure everyone had their favorites. There would be souse meat or ham biscuits, rice pudding, bean cakes, tater cakes, and pickled beans and corn for the dad. No one went hungry.

Mary was the most pleasant fishing buddy, but she would usually skunk everybody by catching more fish than anyone. One day, little sister Roma was fishing so intently when she thought she had a real prize on her line. Mary broke out in laughter and Roma realized she was holding her pole from behind making her think she had a bite! Mary never could control her laughter and several times in church she would have to leave, like one time when a woman's wig fell off.

When Jasper worked for the Forest Service, he would drop Mary and her sister, Icie, off at the Lake, where they would fish all day until Jasper picked them up after work. They would catch enough fish for the family to have a big fish fry.

One morning that is dear to Diamond's heart is when he got up early to go fishing. He went to the spot where his mommy threw out her dish water to get worms for bait. He says that spot grew worms a site! He put them in his backer can (Prince Albert can) and headed for the Snowbird Creek. This was down below their house and as he walked down the trail, his little sister Roma unknowingly followed him.

As he climbed out on the big rock over the Big Hole, all the noise from the house was drowned out from the roar of the creek.

He had cast his line out and watched it go down the stream about three times, when he saw his little sister Roma's petticoat float by. Diamond walked on water that day and just before they both would have been in the dangerous waters, he grabbed Roma! He carried her in his arms, stumbling until he could walk. Holding her so tightly, he suddenly realized how much he loved his baby sister. He knew he would always be her protector and he would always make sure she didn't follow him to the creek anymore. Diamond could have never lived without his little Romee and they will remain close all their lives. Roma has always been afraid of water after that and has never learned to swim.

There were places that were around seven feet deep in the Big Hole. For the little children there was a special little hole about one foot deep on one side to play in. They would return often to fish and swim in the perfect swimming hole that all the Hedricks and Stewarts used it for years. Diamond would practice his preaching skills on his cousins and he would baptize in those waters when he had souls to save.

Diamond Saves Roma

As good as Diamond was, he had a few things he was not proud of. His mommy could always tell when he was smoking rabbit tobacco by looking in his eyes and seeing the yellow. Jasper smoked Prince Albert in the can and Diamond idealized his dad. He would watch so intently as his dad rolled his smokes. He thought this would be a wonderful thing to do, because his dad seemed to enjoy it so much. When Jasper would lay his old butts down, Diamond would snatch them up, not realizing his dad was watching him all the time.

One day, he set him up. After he took a few drags off of a cigarette, he laid it down on the banister. He watched the butt until Diamond picked it up and headed out behind the woodshed. He walked up on him and said, "Now Son, you took the bait, I caught you I don't want you to smoke, but I know you're going to in spite of everything I can do." Now I don't want you bumming, I hate a bum, I'll tell you what I'm going to do. If you do all your choirs and work real hard, I'll buy you a can of Prince Albert a week and a pack of rolling papers. This was the day that would start what became a three pack a day habit for Diamond.

CHAPTER FIFTEEN

Diamond Makes His Mark

Another thing Diamond is not proud of and if Diamond's dad had ever found out about him, Loyd, and Jimtom stealing dopes off the dope truck, he would have skinned them alive. They would hide out at the bottom of Dobson Hill, until they saw the truck coming. Diamond's job to snatch all the orange dopes, Jimtom snatched grape, and Loyd snatched RC. As soon as the truck hit bulldog (1st gear,) they jumped on the back and started their snatching. They would get five or six apiece and head for the cold creek. The man who drove the truck never told on them.

Diamond only got three whippings in his life from his dad. Jasper would never whip his kids when he was mad. He would tell them when they were going to get a whipping and it was always the next day when he got home from work. He never punished when he was mad. Now if he told you that you were going to get one, you could expect it. Set your clock!

Jasper never had spanked Roma, because she was the baby and he let Mary discipline her. Then one night she had boasted to her cousin, Buster, how her dad had never whipped her. Buster told her when her dad fixed her plate as he normally did and asked her what she wanted, tell him "shut up!" That evening Jasper asked Roma what she wanted on her plate. Roma looked at him and said, "Shut up!" Jasper slowly slid his chair back, quietly walked outside, and broke off a hickory. Coming back in he said, "I'm not going to whip you this time, but if you ever do that again, you are going to get a good one!" Now Diamond got whipped often from Mary, whether he needed it or not. Before school she would say, "Now Son, come on out here. We might as well get this over with." All the children of Jasper and Mary Hedrick's would say they were expected to be good and do the right things.

Work had to be done right. Any job that they did Jasper would make sure they did it right or they would have to do it all over again! Jasper would say, "Any job ain't done right, ain't worth doing!" If the haystack wasn't perfectly straight, he'd make them tear it down and go back up with it.

CHAPTER SIXTEEN

Ball Hooting

Ted and Glen Hyde were logging together and they hired fifteen year old Diamond. They logged on Snowbird, Corn Silk, and all around the Carver Cemetery. They paid the young man good back then. Sometimes they would hunt down the chestnut soggs that brought them much more money, especially if it had moss growing on it. A chestnut sogg could not stand direct sunlight, so if you found one in a laurel thicket it was usually a good one. At times logging had to be done on the coldest of times, with three or more inches of snow on the ground. If you were on the side of a mountain, you would do what they call "ball hooting." This was Diamond's favorite way to log. They would cut a notch in the front of a log and slide it off the mountain. If the log got off track, they would use the peeve to roll it where they could slide it through. Sometimes it was a difficult task and the young stubborn Diamond would put his whole body into that peeve. He ended up with a huge hernia on his navel that would embarrass him at times when it would pop out through his clothes. A lot of loggers got these, especially hard working boys. Everything is done with machines today.

Diamond helped his dad with the cross-cut saw, which by any standards is very hard pulling, especially for a fifteen year old boy. Jasper had to make a joke, even knowing he would really hurt Diamond, who was always so eager to please him. As they walked back to the house for dinner, he told Diamond, "Now Son, we'll bring you a saddle back, so you can ride in comfort this evening!" Diamond took it serious and from that day on, he made sure his dad knew he took it serious.

Diamond and Loydd forking hay, and Jasper pruning trees

Jasper always told all his children to stay away from white pines when it came up a storm. The story goes, when Jasper was around eighteen years old he was out in the woods when a lightning storm came up. He sat down under a big white pine to try to stay dry. A big lightning bolt hit the pine and ran through Jasper, addling him. When he became conscious he was miles away from where he got struck. He had nearly ran himself to death!

He also had a lot of very wonderful sayings that came out of a lot of life experiences. Being a woodsman, he knew all about the miracles of this great world that our creator created. He always said he wanted a preacher to preach on nature. If anyone just noticed the life around them and then study about it, you would have to know that there had to be an awesome creator!

Diamond Roach was taken away from Big Snowbird as a young Cherokee Indian boy and came back a professor. He is responsible for building and starting the Indian School. He also taught the Indian children to speak English, while making sure they kept their own language.

He came out to Jasper's on Big Snowbird, looking for a place to build a house. Jasper sold him a place right above him across the road. He built a really good house that was very strong. He built the fireplace in the middle of the house, so it would heat the whole house. The day he was putting his name on his hearth, he came out to get Diamond. Because they had the same name, he wanted to show him how he could make his mark. He poured cement and made it look like a rock. He then scratched out a diamond shape and in the center he put an "R." He then showed him the diamond with an "H" in it for Hedrick. That was the day Diamond would learn to make his mark. He was always a good friend to the Hedrick family.

He taught school a long time on Big Snowbird. When he left there, he sold his place to Diamond's Uncle Leslie. Diamond would use that mark in school and in his business all his life. He would later make this mark on all of his art work.

It was about 1951, when Diamond and his cousin, Vance, went with Rip Lovin to learn how to hunt ginseng. Rip was very much a mountain man, very knowledgeable about the plants and herbs of the mountains. On this day, Rip packed a lunch for the boys and himself. He would make a feast that was of yeast bread, streaked meat, onion, and baked Irish potatoes. Rip Lovin was a real good cook. At this time in his life, he was retired around sixty-five years old. He and his brother lived on Big Snowbird on a big farm. They had beef cattle and grew corn and hay. He and the boys headed out that morning to the head of Sassafras, walking a long way back in the woods, and wading across Big Snowbird Creek.

They were walking along and suddenly when Rip stopped he said, "Come here boys, I see a bunch of ginseng, see if you can find it. I'm going to show you one time and that is the last time I'm going to show you." He told Diamond to go to the left and Vance go to the right, while he went up the middle. Diamond had just walked behind this big rock when he spotted the biggest patch of ginseng with big clusters of red berries. One thing Rip wouldn't do was dig ginseng unless it had red berries. That meant they were ripe enough to plant them back. After Diamond dug his ginseng, he caught back up with Rip. He soon learned to watch Rip when he stopped, he knew there was "Seng."

Then when Rip looked at the sun, he knew it was twelve o'clock and he said, "It's time to eat boys." That picnic lunch sure was good! They had a great time talking with Rip, who had some amazing stories to tell. One story was where he had always wanted to go out west. One day, he left Snowbird and worked his way across the United States. He would work in restaurants, lodges, and motels. When he would get enough money he would go on again and when he ran out he'd get another job until he could go on a little further. He was never satisfied out west. He always missed the Snowbird Mountains. Like so many others that left, Rip came back, and put an end to ever leaving here again.

Soon they went back to finding ginseng again, when Rip suddenly stopped and said, "Boys come here, look there, this is what you have to watch out for." There was the biggest rattle snake the boys had ever seen, coiled up ready to strike! Rip took a stick and struck the snake on the top of its head, killing him instantly. After that, everything that moved scared them, so they quit sengin' early. They started their walk back with the most ginseng they had ever dug in a day. Diamond dug about one pound of green that day.

Every time Rip would make yeast bread, he would invite Diamond and Vance to eat with him. He was such a good cook, but also a very good story teller. They would set in the living room or the kitchen for hours, hanging on every word and learning.

Diamond was a strong, sixteen year old, girl crazy guy. He was strong as an ox and stubborn as well. He was tall with blonde hair and his blue eyes didn't hurt him at all. As much as he liked the girls, they liked him. Every Monday night, he and Vance would go to the movies at the Indian School with some really pretty Indian girls. That's where Diamond had his first kisses and knew he liked it. He says he never did watch the movie. They would walk the girls home after the movie.

Then Diamond and Vance met some girls that were staying at their sisters' on Snowbird. The girl Diamond liked had beautiful brown curls. By this time, he was an experienced kisser and this girl knew how to kiss back. When the girls asked the boys to take them home, all the way out on Hanging Dog forty miles away, they had to find a way.

Vance had just got his driver's license, so they borrowed his daddy's truck. They took them home and it took a long time to get there, because the boys took the scenic route. They were all in the tiny truck seat, jammed packed together, and that never really bothered the couples. The young passionate Diamond was on cloud nine. When they finally got to the girls home, Diamond got an even better kiss saying goodnight on her front porch.

Before leaving them, the boys asked for another date for the following week. The next weekend, they went to their house to pick them up. After going in and talking to their parents for a while, they asked if they could go riding around with them. Their parents said not to keep them out too late. With the girls in the truck, they went to the closest parking spot. The boys were just boys, and boys will be boys and girls will be girls.

Diamond and Vance would keep going back, until one night after dropping the girls off, they were met by some Hanging Dog boys who didn't like them dating these girls. These boys pulled in behind them and tried to pass them, catching their bumper and pulling it off onto the road. Diamond told Vance not to run, "We got to hold our ground. Whether you want to come back or not, we got to stand our ground." Vance said, "Oh, I want to come back." Vance stopped the truck but the boys kept right on going.

The cousins went back to the girl's house and told them what happened. They decided the girls would have to come back to their sisters house on Snowbird if they wanted to see them again. The girls lasted for about six months, then the boys got interested in other girls. Vance would soon get married to Waynell Adams.

Diamond Hedrick Sophomore

CHAPTER SEVENTEEN

Bad Behavior

Diamond would soon link up with his other cousin, Junior Stewart, when Vance got married. They got to drinking moonshine and were both getting drunk a lot. Mary was always two steps ahead of them and she could not be fooled. Diamond would get into her kraut juice when he would have a hangover. The next morning she asked, "Now Son, do you think I don't know what you are doing with my kraut juice?" One night, Diamond and Junior came home so drunk and tried to slip quietly into the house. They realized Mary had put a chair in front of the door, so that she would know they got home. All night the bed rolled and rolled, and the boys took on something terrible. Mary came in and said,"Younses get up and put younses feet on the floor!" They set up for the rest of the night.

One very worried weekend for Mary was when the boys were gone three days and she had no clue where they were. Mary and Jasper, along with Junior's Mom and Dad, had their own search party in the woods and around all the lakes. These were two very worried families. They sure didn't know their sixteen year old sons were sowing the wild oats with some women they met in Tennessee. When they came home, Diamond's brand new clothes smelled so bad with that rotten moonshine, and other unmentionable smells, that Mary had to carry them on a stick outside to burn them.

That hurt Diamond so bad when he realized how he had worried his mommy and he had learned that lesson well. He loved her and that kind of behavior would never happen again!

There was a real pretty girl who lived at Snowbird Mountain Lodge, where her mom and dad worked. She had long blonde curls and she was a picture of beauty. She was such a nice girl and Diamond thought he might be falling in love. Up until then, it was more of a puppy love, but this felt like the real thing. He started to think she was someone he wanted to marry.

At first, Junior liked her and wanted Diamond to talk to her parents for him. Junior did not have the confidence to talk to them, he wasn't quite the talker Diamond was. Diamond and this girl knew each other from school, so while he was in her house they had come to the conclusion they really liked each other. He had no trouble talking to her parents, only not for Junior, but for himself. Junior did not like this, but this was something Diamond could not help.

He would spend a lot of time at the lodge with her, but when her mom and dad had to move out to Texas, this beautiful little romance had to end. Diamond missed her and was heartsick for a while. It didn't take him long to climb back up again and soon there were other nice girls he would date. Diamond said that cured that!

There were a lot of beautiful girls in Diamond's class and he had crushes on all of them. All of the boys were crazy in love with a beautiful girl named Joyce Stratton. She was so smart and so charismatic. Diamond was always trying to be near her, especially after lunch. That was when she had to redo her lipstick. Diamond had the honor of holding her mirror for her and then she let him blot her lips on his lips! It was such a thrill, but he never dated her, because he never had the confidence to ask her out, even though he wanted to date her so bad.

He loved sitting by her in class and because she was so smart, he would sometimes copy her paper. One day they were taking a big important test. Question number eight had even Joyce stumped and she wrote, "I don't know." Well Diamond wrote on his paper, "Me neither." His teacher Tom Carpenter caught him and told him he better never copy her paper again. This is a joke Diamond tells everyone! Not so sure it's a true story. Joyce always looked so striking marching onto the field in her Drum Majorette uniform. He also loved to watch her play basketball and like everything she did, she was best!

Mildred Jordan was another girl Diamond had a big crush on. She was a very friendly outgoing girl who was also very beautiful. Wanda Garland was a wonderful and very nice girl. She was also a very pretty girl. Another beautiful girl he had a crush on was a real good basketball player, was Dorothy Farley.

Diamond had a big crush on Edith Atwell, she was a lot of fun. He used to go to the ball game with her and sometimes go down to her Mother's house to see her. Louise Crisp and Virginia Bridges were girls that were lot of fun and so nice to be around. Wanda Roberts and Estell Waldroup were real good friends. All of these women were all so beautiful and highly thought of by Diamond and he always valued their friendships.

With all the school years, the list of special wonderful girls keeps on going. Kay and Leunia Mahaffee were sisters that were so special to Diamond. Ollean and Betty Sawyer were sisters that were his good friends. Another special friend who he really had a close friendship to was Waynell Adams. Arlene Crisp has always been a good friend. He remembers her being a hard worker. Another very smart girl who Diamond says always tried to help him in his studies, was Billie Ann Millsaps. He also wanted to date Barbara Huskinson, but they just stayed close friends.

D.R. Wildes was probably Diamond's favorite teacher who taught him in the eighth grade. He always noticed how good Diamond could kick a football. He would let the whole class go with him to football practice every evening to watch the High School boys practice. One day, he called Diamond out onto the field and said, "Diamond show these boys how to punt." Diamond did well that day to impress and the coach said, "Now boys, that's how it's done!"

The whole class loved this teacher. One day in the classroom he made a challenge to Diamond, knowing what a good horse shoe player he was and a good punter, he bet he could beat him. He told the class if Diamond beat him they wouldn't have to work the next day and they could play all day, but if he won he would work them to death. Diamond and the class just knew he could beat him. The class was cheering for Diamond and everyone was excited until Mr. Wildes kicked the football. It went full the length of the field. Diamond's went about forty yards and his went eighty. Diamond can never forget that little grin on his face. He then said, "Let's go up to the horse shoe pits and you go first." First one Diamond threw was a dead ringer, everyone went wild! Next one was a leaner worth 3 points, that was 9 points. They just knew he couldn't beat that. The teacher threw 2 ringers for 12 points and that made the class so mad at Diamond. They had to work the next day and didn't get recess.

One bad day at school a big kid started bulling a little kid and started beating up on him, causing Mr. Wildes to have to separate them. That evening Mr. Wildes heard a knock on his door and when he answered that boy's dad shot him almost killing him. He would be out for around two months and a substitute took over until his return. The class all missed him so much, especially Diamond. The day finally came when they looked out and saw him coming down the hill. They all started hollering and shouting, and when he joined them in the classroom he realized how much they had missed him, he was overwhelmed with emotion and broke down and cried.

Then when Diamond was in the tenth grade he started playing football for the Robbinsville Blue Devils. Coach Wildes was his coach and he had a special position in mind for Diamond. Punting was what Diamond loved and he was thrilled. Life was hard, but oh so good. Diamond was the punter for a whole year, then in the 11th grade things would change. Coach Wildes moved away and this was very upsetting to Diamond, but he always knew he was a better person for knowing D.R. Wildes.

Diamond knew the new coach, Modell Walsh and he and Modell were very good buddies. He made Diamond a lineman and that meant he had to play both defense and offense. By the time the game was over, he was so tired he could hardly move. The team would go straight to the showers after a game and this would be relaxing to their many aching muscles. They would wash away the stinky sweat and the horrendous mud splattered all over their hair, faces, and bodies. They would leave the dressing room ready for action and starved to death.

The school took the team for hamburgers and french fries after the game. That's when Diamond first became obsessed with The Junaluska Grill and Ma Woods Café. They were both wonderful places for young people to meet and converse with the opposite sex and they put many coins into the juke boxes. It was 1957-1958 and Fats Domino had a big hit back then called Blueberry Hill. Some other artists that were his favorites were Chuck Berry, Little Richard, and The Everly Brothers. This was very exciting music for the boys and girls to play on the juke box. Back then, every booth or table had a little box that played the juke box. You could put nickels, dimes, and quarters in and your song would be in the lineup. They played for a nickel a piece, but if you put a quarter in it played six.

They were allowed to smoke in the irestaurants and back then and there was an ashtray on every table. Most of the boys smoked, but not many of the girls did. At school there was a smoking ring drawn on the ground and they had to be inside the circle when they smoked. Eventually they poured a tar and gravel paved pad for them to stand on. Diamond would roll Prince Alberts at night for the next school day. He always rolled plenty, enough to last all day. He liked the fact they looked like tailor made. He had to buy a special cigarette paper with stick'um on the back, so they would last all day.

In the summer months on school break Diamond would always get in great shape from practicing football early every morning. He built a strong back and thigh muscles from the many hours working on their farm, as well. He and Vincent Waldroup would usually start out walking and thumbing to football practice. They would usually get picked up by some loggers or somebody that was going in or out of Snowbird if they were lucky. After practice, another walk home was a very tough seven miles and in Vincent's case it was eight miles. Thank goodness everybody knew them and they didn't have to walk it many times, because there was always farm work to be done when they got home. Diamond was already a young logger that they all knew and he was getting to know all the loggers personally.

One day Diamond's coach, Modell Walsh, brought his prize fighting cock to school and wanted Diamond to take care of him at his house. That evening they worked on a pen and fixed it good enough to hold this rooster Coach Walsh had paid a lot of money for. Diamond's dad had a giant Dominicker rooster that just ran loose. While Diamond was at school one day, the cock got out and tried to cut in on the **Dominicker's** hens. When Diamond got home, he hurried back to feed Modell's rooster, he found a very bloody rooster that his dad had to finish killing. The Dominicker remained unscathed. Diamond dreaded giving Modell the bad news. He didn't expect to hear him laugh about it, but he did. He said, "Well Diamond I'm not glad, but I'd lost a lot of money if he couldn't fight any better than that."

This was a fun time for a poor boy from Snowbird. He was always glad he cried when he started the first grade. After returning home his mom and dad let him stay home another year to mature a bit. Because of this he was put with the greatest class he could ever be with! Diamond was the first one of seven to graduate in his family. He probably owes a lot to his wonderful friends. They have always been close to his heart.

CHAPTER EIGHTEEN

Diamond Gets Married

When Diamond was twenty one he was working with Ted logging, when he met his wife to be, Shirley Turpin. He was standing with a group of his friends when Shirley came by and waved to him from the backseat of her double first cousins car. Diamond had to see the girl who was in the backseat of this car. He didn't get far when he saw the car parked in front of Phillip's Restaurant.

Diamond found a seat beside Shirley and confidently sit down. Diamond said, "When you waved at me I had to find out who you were." Shirley told Diamond she had had her eyes on him a long time. That was how it started. He was very attracted to Shirley and she was very attracted to him. Diamond was involved with another girl and had moved in with her, their relationship had not been right for some time and Shirley was what he had been looking for. He went back home to his parent's house that night and never returned to that relationship, not even to get his clothes. After they dated for about three months, he drove Shirley up on Robbinsville Mountain to a very much used parking place and proposed to her. Shirley said he would have to ask her dad for her hand.

That morning when he drove out to Yellow Creek to fetch his bride, he was so nervous that before going into the house he lit a cigarette, threw the cigarette down, and took a puff on the match! He never got the nerve to ask her dad and it took Shirley a long time to get ready. It was Halloween and they got Edward and Arbutus Hollifeild to go with them to be their witnesses. They honeymooned in Bryson City in a little motel that night. Diamond and Shirley were so happy to start their life together and they returned the next day to move in with Shirley's mom and dad on Yellow Creek.

Shirley's dad asked Diamond the most important thing he wanted to know, what his politics were. Diamond told him Republican and a big smile came across his face and he said, "We are going to get along just fine." They always got along fine, until one day he asked Diamond to rob his bees. Diamond told him that was one thing he would not do and if he had to he could just have her back! That tickled him to death and he never asked him to do that again.

Diamond would learn a real good lesson about a woman's cooking one evening when he came in from work. Shirley spooned out some beans on his plate. He looked at the plate of beans and happened to say out loud, "Mommy's always had a little soup in hers." That's when Shirley dumped all the hot beans on Diamond's head and all over the kitchen. He would never made that mistake again!

The most important day in Diamonds life was when he found out he was going to be a father, he was the happiest man alive! He loved babies so much all his life and now he would have his own. Nine months later, their son was born. Shirley had a hard time having the baby and nearly bled to death. The doctor told them they shouldn't have anymore. They named him Stephen Scott Hedrick and were the most doting parents around. Everybody was so happy for the couple.

At that time they were living in Sniderville and the rent was so high. Diamond could not afford it, so they moved into the little house in Sleepy Hollow that Grandma Freddie lived in. After Grandpa Pose died, Jasper and all the Hedrick brothers remodeled a small building that was John's can house for Grandma Freddie. They made the cutest little house for her so she could be next door to John and Maggie and their children.

Diamond loved being near his little Grandma and close to his family. Jasper and Mary always wanted them to live on Snowbird Creek. Diamond's dad took him a side one day and showed him what he wanted to give to him. It was the old home place where Diamond grew up. It was still a beautiful farm with apple orchard, barn, and most important of all, the beautiful Snowbird Creek. Diamond remembered his youth living in the old house. It was a board roof that the rain never came in, but when it snowed they would wake up with a light powdering of snow on their cover. Mary would tuck him and Loyd in at night and she would tell them to get the way they wanted to be because when she got through they wouldn't be moving. Mary would pin their quilt to the sheets. He pictured a life there for him and Shirley, where they would be forever happy. There was just one big problem with all of this, it was not what Shirley wanted. Shirley had lived in the back woods all her life and she did not want this for her home. Diamond sadly walked away from that dream. Shirley was never happy and Diamond always joked that he tried to buy her the court house lawn, but they wouldn't sell it. No matter where he moved her, eventually she was unhappy.

Roma was fifteen years old when she met the young and very handsome, Hugh Atwell. She was one of the cutest teenage girls around. She wasn't allowed to date yet and being the baby in the family didn't help either. Diamond let her and Hugh meet at their house to do their courting. Then one day Roma and Hugh asked Diamond and Shirley to help them get married. They knew their dad and mom would not allow this. Mommy had a special saying when she really meant no. "No iser about it!"

Being only sixteen, Roma had to have someone to sign for her, so Diamond would have too. Diamond knew Hugh would be a good man for Roma and he didn't have a problem signing. When they went before the Murphy magistrate and he asked why her parents couldn't sign for her, Diamond told him Mommy had to take care of the babies. That was such a lie, because Roma was the baby. Jasper and Mary were so furious at Diamond and did not let him come around.

Eventually they found out what a good man Hugh was and welcomed Diamond back into the fold. Hugh and Roma would have one daughter, Rockanne, a beautiful little strawberry blonde. She was every bodies little pet and the apple of Hugh and Roma's eye. They called her Rocky.

Life was almost perfect, until one day, Diamond had a terrible accident. He was working on a truck that was up on blocks putting the center bolts in, when it slipped off. Diamond was lying on his side and the truck landed on his shoulder, crushing his chest so hard that he couldn't breathe. Ted had gone into town with Mary and Jasper and while they went to the market he went to buy the tires for this truck. Diamond was alone and was almost dead when they got back. Jasper picked up the truck that day and Ted pulled Diamond out.

They took him to the clinic in Mill Town, where he saw Dr. Dick Perett, who tried to put his shoulder back in place. He decided to wait a couple of days to see if he improved. Diamond didn't have health insurance, so he put off treatment. When he could no longer stand it and he was not improving, he went to Mission Memorial Hospital. There they x-rayed it and saw it had not grown back right. They said they would have to break it again so it would be better to leave it alone. Diamond couldn't work for nearly a year and became so depressed. His dad signed a bank note for him to get money for his family to live on. They had a hard time getting by, but with the help of all the Hedricks', they survived.

When Diamond was healed, he worked for Thunderbird Resort, putting in septic lines for seventy-five cents an hour. Later, he took a job with Daniel Construction, building the new Burlington Carpet Mill that would later become Burlington Furniture Plant. He still made seventy-five cents an hour. When he finished this job he went up the railroad tracks to work for Bemis Lumber Company, still making seventy-five cents an hour. Then President, Dwight D. Eisenhower, raised the minimum wage to one dollar an hour and froze all prices.

CHAPTER NINETEEN

High Cotton

Shirley and Diamond thought they were in high cotton. They were buying everything from Snowbird Supply, owned by Bemis Lumber Company. Life was good for the Diamond Hedrick's. He really loved this job, because he got to work with his Uncle John, who he admired so much.

John had been bit by a Copperhead while hunting ginseng and he opened up his own finger and sucked out the poison. Diamond always looked up to him and loved working with him. They worked with a road crew building bridges, and he loved building the many bridges with his Uncle John.

Diamond was tired of renting from Bemis and wanted to own his own home. He and Shirley went to a Mobile Home Sales in Andrews and talked to Ruby Curtis. She was a Robbinsville girl who married an Andrews man, Harold Curtis, and started their own Mobile Home Sales. She was a really easy person to deal with and she made sure they got their down payment by taking their furniture in on a trade. Diamond always admired the business woman she was and always knew if he had a business he would want to help people like she did. He put this home on Eller Branch and Jasper helped put in a septic tank. It also turned out Ruby was Joyce Stratton's sister.

Then about two years later, Diamond and Shirley went back to the mobile home sales again and found another deal on a double wide repossession. They bought it "as is," needing to be cleaned up. Cleo Smith gave them a place in Mill Town to put their new home. Cleo was a real good friend and he wanted Diamond to live by him. Diamond sold his place on Eller branch and made his new home place into a beautiful place. He even invented a screen door for his sliding glass door. Diamond felt a real since of pride in his new home and life was perfect. He then planted some peach trees, apple trees, and pear trees. He also planted a fine garden.

Diamond was scaling logs for Bemis Saw Mill, when they made a request he simply would not do. His boss told him to give a forty percent overrun when the scale stick gives ten, he was mortified! This would have hurt all the loggers and their families, and Diamond knew these families. They told him if he couldn't do that, he could go home. Diamond walked off by two o'clock that day and by six o'clock he had nearly three hundred men in his yard. They were all showing their support by refusing to take another load of logs to Bemis.

It was the biggest piece of news to hit Graham County in a long time. Many people lost their jobs, because they refused to work for Bemis. Diamond was on the six o'clock news on the Asheville channel and had a story in The Graham Star and The Asheville Citizen. He also talked to Congressman Roger West and he said he would see what could be done. Diamond said if he had to do wrong to keep his job, he wouldn't do that. The State checked all the logs Diamond had scaled for a year and it came out 9.9 percent. Roger West said that was as close as anyone could get to 10 percent. Still, nothing could be done and Bemis shut down.

Diamond headed out on the coast of North Carolina and South Carolina when Hurricane Hugo destroyed so much property. This was cleanup work with a lot of long hard hours for Diamond. He was used to hard work and after what he'd been through, he loved the chance to get away. His boss was Bluford Carpenter and he was a real good friend. He and his wife, Bea, shared their meals with Diamond. Bea was a real good cook and made really good coffee. She would make the thousand things Diamond liked, pinto beans. She also fried real good chicken, Diamond's favorite. It didn't hurt having a Kentucky Fried Chicken next door either, that's his favorite.

A funny story Diamond tells on his mommy is her having to take her to an Optometrist in Franklin. There were several good places to eat, but Mary said she had never wanted a piece of Kernel's chicken so bad in all her life, which was odd because

Mary never ate chicken in her life. After getting her meal she gave her chicken to Diamond and ate only the fixings. She knew how her boy loved chicken.

Diamond was on the coast for three months working twelve hours a day, seven days a week. One day, he was so lonesome and missing his home so bad, he looked up and saw his best friend Bill Pruett coming toward him. Bill thought he was seeing a ghost, he says he never saw anyone as sad as that. Diamond would finally make it back home and never had to leave again.

When he got home a new company had bought Bemis. E.M. Nesmith had bought the mill and he met with Diamond on his porch and asked him to come work for them. Diamond was tickled to death. This job lasted about two years and they were a good company to work for. It seemed they were just there long enough to sell the existing lumber. Then, the company decided to auction everything off, land included. Diamond knew he had to act fast to continue working and to help the loggers stay around.

Diamond's dream was to have his own log yard, so he could scale the way he wanted to without somebody looking down his neck. Diamond wanted to keep all the loggers working, but not just to be working. Diamond wanted them to be treated fair and he would be able to do that now. He knew he could never do this endeavor alone, he needed a partner and Tim Roberts was the good friend to fit the bill.

Together they put together the finest business that Robbinsville would ever know. The log yard was the place to be, even when they had bad days and the loggers had no logs. The loggers all had a place to meet and talk about all their subjects, including politics.

Diamond and Tim, strong republicans, didn't much care how you talked about it as long as they agreed! Diamond would get up and give his political speeches. The men hung on every word. All the young sons of the loggers cut their teeth at the yard. They learned a lot listening to the men and riding the loader with Diamond. The kids all called him "Papaw Diamond." They even named the loader "Ole Satan." Diamond loved his life at the yard and he and Tim made good livings.

Diamond and Shirley sold their home and went out the street and bought a house that needed a lot of work. Diamond handled all this, all the while they made sure all the loggers were treated fair and square.

The problem that they had was when they paid a truck to haul their logs to Sylva, Old Fort, and Chattanooga, Tennessee. They were always getting in trouble with the weight and lengths division. At the last of every month they were having to pay heavy fines. Congressman Roger West went before the General Assembly and spoke out for the logging industry. Roger West said, "If you fellers put out a load and someone took everything you had, you would change this law!" They allowed a trucker eighty- eight thousand pounds for a load of chips, because they were a finish product. A load of logs only got eighty thousand pounds per load, because they were not a finish product. This didn't make sense, but it was the way it was and still is.

Ronnie Roberts and Grand Daughter Lexie

CHAPTER TWENTY

Bad Log

Diamond had some really good logging friends that lost their lives through the years. The most recent happened the other day when a log rolled off the top onto his best friend, Ronnie Robinson, landing on his hip. He was able to call 911 on his cell phone and then called his wife, Deb. He told the 911 operator the log was off of him.

When his cousin Billie Lewis and Deb got there, the log was still on him. Ronnie told Deb to get his dinner bucket. Deb told Ronnie, "Ronnie, you don't need that right now." After they had all looked for the check that Dalton had just wrote him, Deb looked in the lunch box and found the check. He was transported by helicopter to U.T. and eight minutes after they got him in the air he passed away, going to Heaven for sure. Very sad day in everyone's life. He was loved by everyone and will be missed forever. His son Chase Robinson will probably take up in a few years where his dad left off.

John Chickelel had an accident when he took the chains off a load of logs and a log rolled off the top. He was trying to get away when he tripped on the log behind him and he was crushed between the two logs.

The hardest thing Diamond ever had to do was get a log off of his good friend, Paul Orr. A small log came off the top, straight down hitting him in the head, and driving him into the ground. Diamond has a very hard time re-living this. The tragedy didn't end there for the family, because their son Harold was killed when a tractor turned over on him.

Emit Sherill and his dad brought Diamond a load of logs one morning and said they would see him after a while. When they went back to work Diamond got word a tractor had turned over on Emit, killing him. Dale Evans was trying to dislodge a tree that stuck in another tree, when the tree came crashing down on top of him. He died instantly. David Peterson was down below hooking logs, when a fellow cutting above him cut a tree that fell on him. He didn't see him and it was such a tragic accident.

Ed Waldroup married Diamond's mother's double first cousin. His sons and Diamond were real good buddies. Ed was hooking tongs in a big pile of logs, when as soon as he hooked one and they pulled it out, it turned another one loose that rolled over on him. He was killed instantly and never knew what hit him. When the load came to the log yard, Diamond unloaded a log that they had wrote "BAD LOG!" on. That was the log that killed poor Ed. Diamond put that one straight through to the mill. Nobody wanted to see that log anymore.

Troy Waldroup was Ed's brother. Troy was logging with his son, Phillip, when Troy hooked the tongs in a log. Phillip picked it up with a stiff neck loader and the boom broke sending it crashing on top of Troy, killing him.

So many men came close to getting killed in the logging trade back then. Diamond had a lot of close calls himself. A window maker came down and as Diamond broke to run a saw briar fowled him, causing his big Poulland chain saw to rip across his leg, tearing out chunks of flesh. He still wears a scar and the memory of that day.

Another time, Diamond learned a lesson the hard way. He was trimming a limb, when he cut the tip off the bent tree and it came back and stuck him across the bridge of his nose, right square between his eyes. Through all the sadness and dangers, there were some real friendships forged. A really strong friendship for Diamond were the Lewis men.

CHAPTER TWENTY ONE

The Lewis Brothers

Hardwood Lewis said there was three sides to every story, "Your side, their side, and the right side." Diamond says he was the toughest man he ever knew. Don't never cross him! Diamond, Junior Stewart, and Hardwood were drinking on the tail gate of a big log truck when the sheriff, Boyd Crisp, and a highway patrolman, Buck Boyles, pulled up. They started to arrest Hardwood for being drunk. He told them, "I promised Mommy I'd be home tonight and I must go." They tried to handcuff him, but they couldn't do anything with him, so they didn't arrest him. Diamond told them he would take him home to his mommy and they let him go.

Hardwood eventually married Nettie Eller and they had two girls and four boys. They also had two babies die soon after being born, Mark and Melanie. Diabetes hit their family hard. Hardwood died young, as well as sons Marty and Darren. His son, Mike, has had such a struggle all his life having to have a kidney transplant some years back. Mike is also one of the many Robbinsville men to appear on the television show, "Moonshiners."

Diamond always thought of Hardwood's children as his own after Hardwood died. One son, Andy, helped Diamond in his business with the many mechanic jobs, as well as bringing in many loads of Logs. Hardwood's two fine daughters are Misty Emory and Pam Williams, and they have made the best mothers. All of Hardwood's Grandchildren, Diamond thinks as his own.

Hardwood's brother, Delmas Lewis, was another good logging friend. One of the best timber cutters and the best log hauler around. He was a Jack of all trades. He raised a fine family with his wife, Sue Robinson Lewis. His son Joe was such a jokester and a lot of fun, always smiling. Joe had a son who Diamond has always thought of as his own son, David. Joe Lewis died so young, while having a liver transplant.

21-A Smiling Joe Lewis on the knuckle boom

David is a truck driver now. Joe also has a younger brother, Billy, who is one of the best family men around and he owns an upholstery shop and is very good at his work. He also works for Veach- Wilson Oil Company. Delmas and Sue adopted one of the sweetest little girls name Patsy, who Diamond's family claims as their niece. She is a dispatcher for the county. Perhaps the best friend of all the brothers is James Lewis, he grew up with Diamond and when Diamond's dad was pulling teeth at home, James ran like a turkey with Diamond! Diamond unloaded more logs off of James than anybody. He was fearless and unstoppable. He was bringing in a big load of logs one day, when the steering wheel came off. The fearless James found a set of vice- grip pliers and steered that truck into the log yard. He still to this day is one of Diamond's closest friends.

Diamond doesn't want to leave anyone out, if somehow he does, he did not mean to overlook them, it's just hard to remember all the names. A very skilled tree climber we can't forget on the list is Mark Rogers, of the famous "Moonshiners" show. Just like a squirrel, he flies through the trees, hooking ropes, and cutting limbs off. He is another really good friend and second cousin of Diamond's.

A fellow, Greg Grindstaff who everyone calls Peanut, tells us his story about going logging with his dad, Doyle Grindstaff, and his Uncle. When he was an infant it was necessary to go with them sometimes when his momma had to work. When they rolled him up in a blanket, he reminded them of a peanut, hence forth he was called "Peanut." They usually put him and his bottle of milk on the dash of the truck to keep both warm. He made a fine logger. With all these loggers, their families, and so many friends that the log yard was home away from home to! Their kids could always find a treat, candy, or apple. Diamond and Tim always kept cakes, cookies, and candy for everyone. It was a kind a pay if you want to situation. They kept grate fruits, apples, and peaches. Probably a million cups of coffees were made there. Soft drinks were always in the refrigerator. Of course, Diamond always kept his favorite, bologna. Every morning, he and Mark Rogers made a big breakfast for the men that needed it.

Diamond had a lot of friends that would at some time visit him. Eric Rudoulf as a man that a lot of people liked. He would come from time to time and Diamond would give him Hemlock bark to build bird houses with. Of course, everyone knows he went on to do very bad stuff. One day, he pulled into the log yard and brought Diamond a beautiful birdhouse. It was hard to believe such a seemingly nice man could have committed the crimes he did.

CHAPTER TWENTY TWO

Diamond Loses His Best Friends

With all of Diamond's problems and troubles, he enjoyed a full life with his family. Mary was always getting everyone together to go fishing or on picnics. All through those years, Mary was the loving wife and mother. She really enjoyed her life. Everyone remembers her showing up out of the blue to go fishing with poles and a lunch packed. How could they ever refuse her? As well as her children she loved her son's wives, her daughter's husbands, and really loved her grandchildren.

Mary was around seventy-four when she got sick with too much ammonia in her blood. Two of her brothers had the same condition. She was put on a strict diet and she lost too much weight. She did everything the doctor ordered, even started walking every day. It seemed to work against her and the ammonia overtook her body.

Marvin's wife, Gladys, came every morning and helped the very frail Mary. She did the cooking, washing, and straightened the house. She did everything she could to help out. Mary's family had to choose to give or not to give a medicine that would prolong her life, but would take away her memory. They could not stand her not knowing them, so they chose not to.

Monday evening, when Diamond got in from work, Roma told him on the phone he better come see his mom. He had been with her all weekend and she had not shown one sign of knowing anyone. When he got there, he sat down on the bed and the nurse told him he couldn't sit on the bed. Diamond told the nurse, "Yes I can, that's my Mommy!" Diamond held her hand and held her against him, and said, "Now Mommy, you're going to talk to me. If you know who I am squeeze my hand, Mommy!" She responded with a grunt. Diamond felt her squeeze his hand and then he felt the life leave her. Mary went to her Heavenly home.

Diamond felt so blessed for being there to hold his precious mommy and so glad he went back that night. He also appreciated his great friend, Tim Roberts, for taking him that night.

Jasper was very lost after she died and every day he went to the cemetery and worked on her grave. He only lived four years after Mary. Jasper Fulton Hedrick, born September 12th, 1906, died March 24th, 1996. Mary Ann Stewart Hedrick, born February 15, 1913, died December 17, 1992. They are buried in the Carver Cemetery on West Buffalo.

Two weeks after Mary died, Diamond went back to the house late in evening. He walked up to the front door, opening it he walked in. There his Mommy stood like she always had and said, "come on in and eat supper." After Diamond sat down, she stood behind him, lifting the plate of chicken and dumplings over and down in front of him. Then everything disappeared. Whether you believe this or not isn't important to Diamond. The only one, until now, who knows this is me and I believe this 100%. Just for the record, I do believe in ghosts. Diamond has never gotten over losing his mommy.

Diamond buried himself in his work, which was his life. All the loggers looked up to him for his guidance. They were still heavily involved in many conversations about politics and Diamond still got up in front of all the men with his strong conservative opinions. In Robbinsville, where separation of church and state seems mineable at best. The church keeps the politics conservative. All the men loved and respected Diamond and Tim for their strong conservative views. It was very busy at the log yard. Diamond and Tim were doing good in their business and all the loggers were happy. It was a big happy family, until one day a phone call would end it all.

CHAPTER TWENTY THREE

Life Changes Again

Diamond's wife called so very upset and crying with the news she had just learned. She had ovarian cancer. James and Tim were there and they told Diamond they would handle things at the yard and he should go home. Diamond went home to the most pitiful sight he had ever seen. She did not want their son, Steve, to know until he got home so she could tell him in person. He was coming home that weekend to take a vacation with his mom and dad to Ohio.

Plans changed and everyone was devastated. Steve was an only child and very close to Shirley. He was the only child she could ever have and she had always kept him close. He was his mommy's boy, just like Diamond was his mommy's boy.

When Steve was just a little boy, age six, they almost lost him to Brits Disease. This is where your kidneys stop removing the poison out of your body and you really swell with all the poisons that are not being filtered anymore. The Doctor told Diamond's mother he probably wouldn't live, because most children don't survive it.

Nobody told Shirley or Diamond until he did survive and he got better. For a whole year of his life, he couldn't attend school so his teacher, Mrs. Nora Turner, would come every day to bring his lessons for that day. Steve was a smart boy and never got behind. It was a really wonderful thing his teacher did for them. Shirley and Diamond had to make sure for a whole year he didn't move very much and that was very hard. With all this dedication they made it through.

Now his little mommy has her own illness to go through. Their vacation would have to wait, because Shirley had an appointment with a cancer doctor on Monday. After doing Shirley's exam, the doctor called them all into the office. They would all find out that day, Shirley had stage four ovarian cancer. Their world just exploded in front of them, especially Steve's. Diamond had to be the strong one for his family that was so devastated.

The doctor said she would need to be operated on pretty quickly. Shirley told him she would like to go back to Nashville one more time before they operate. He told her if she thought she could stand it, she could. She said she could, so they all went home and packed for Nashville.

They stayed two nights and all they did was worry, so they headed back home, and Shirley would have what would be her first surgery in Asheville. She had to stay in the hospital for a week after surgery. Then Steve brought her and Diamond to his home in Asheville to stay for two weeks to get her chemotherapy started. That was the worst thing Shirley ever went through in her whole life. Diamond was the most loving, patient man a woman could ever have to go through anything with. He was the energizer bunny, he took a liking and kept on ticking! For two weeks, she had chemotherapy and every day and Diamond did everything for her. She wouldn't let him out of her sight. He had to start a whole new life of bed pans, feeding, everything a home aid worker would do.

When they went back home to Robbinsville, Shirley had to go into the nursing home until Diamond got a handicap ramp built and everything else she would need in place. Diamond had to stay with her all the time and because she wouldn't eat the nursing home cooking he would walk down the hill to their house, close by to make her favorite breakfast. She always wanted the same things; two pancakes with strawberries and one boiled egg.

Diamond's skilled brothers started working on the ramp immediately. Diamond was glad to be home and looked forward to watching his brothers build the ramp for Shirley. He just got to watch a short time, when the nursing home called saying she was in a lot of pain and wanted him there. The pain got worse and worse, and they called for the ambulance. Diamond would have to take another ride to Sylva in the back of the ambulance with Shirley, or she would have refused to go.

At the hospital, they met with a kidney doctor and he explained she needed a tube to go from her kidney to her bladder. This would have to be done all over again every three months. After this surgery and short stay in the hospital, Diamond brought her home to a terrible surprise. Their whole ceiling had come down in their kitchen, because of the huge amount of rain that they had. Diamond did the best job he could by himself. He managed to put the old ceiling back up and got up on the roof and tried to patch it, but every time he would climb back up she would holler for him.

Diamond and Tim already had talked about selling the business and had done so some time back. He was able to walk away and help his wife, but he was missing it so bad and regret had set in. Right now he had to fix things in his house.

The rain just kept on coming and soon they had to go back to the hospital to have her surgery again. While Diamond was at the hospital he got worried about his house, because it was still raining. He had never seen it rain so hard. He called his nephew, Michael Shuler, to go check his house.

Michael called back and said there was no way to patch it and it would need a whole new roof. Diamond told him he couldn't do that, he had too many hospital bills. Michael told Diamond he would take it up at church, because they like to help people that way. After they got home, one Friday they looked out to see a truck arriving at their house. Shirley laid in her bed and counted, as thirty men went up the latter. In one day they totally covered the house in plywood and put on the new metal roof.

Daniel Stewart, the preacher at Cedar Cliff, led the brigade and brought his dump truck to help out. Michael and Ronnie Shuler, Jack Jackson, Bobbie McGuire, BD Royal, Calvin Bridges, David Holder, Hugh Atwell, Dennis Orr, Lennox, Loyd, and Ted Hedrick, Dennis Carey, Earl Watts, Roger Adams, and many more. They worked hard and got it done!

They didn't get to be home long, when The Cancer Center called and wanted to try a new experimental treatment. After arriving in Asheville, Diamond was told at the desk he couldn't go in with her for this consultation. They took Shirley back and while she was in the restroom getting a urine sample she fell, blocking the door. They couldn't get it open, so they had to take it down. Shirley should never have been left to do that unassisted and Diamond should have sued them.

One thing about Diamond is, he would never sue anybody. He certainly wouldn't sue a place that might cure his wife! Now, because of their mistake, Diamond and Shirley could not go home that day. They would stay in a hospital room and the nursing home for the next three months.

Shirley would not let the nurses and the aids do anything for her, she left this all to Diamond. She hollered for him all the time. He could not leave her side when she was awake at all. If she was asleep and he left for a cup of coffee, she would wake up and he could hear her yelling for him. When they finally went home, a home health nurse would come to give her therapy to try and help her walk. Shirley didn't try very hard, because she was trying to give up.

The next three years, Shirley and Diamond went through some really hard times together. Diamond had to do things he couldn't imagine in his wildest dreams. Unclogging her kidney tube, keeping it clean, and washing her sheets every day. Dressing, bathing, feeding, helping on and off the commode. Taking her to appointments and one long hospital stay after another.

Diamond had cancer in his eye through all this and couldn't see his own storm coming up the tracks. Finally, he had to let Novella take over for him for a while, when he and Roma headed out to Peachtree to have the cancer removed from his left eye. Thank God they had got all the cancer and that was the best news he had in a long time. They were able to go home that night and Diamond was back on the job, taking care of Shirley.

One very bad night in their life, Diamond couldn't get her kidney tube open and after he had gone as far as he could go, he called 911. When they came, Diamond was rolling her around the house as her last request. She said she knew she would never be back. She wanted to see her home one more time. They took that ambulance ride one more time and they would be at the hospital for twenty-three days.

The day before Shirley passed away, Diamond was so tired and worn out. He had been on call for four years and he could barely make it. Steve had come into the room and Diamond said he had to go get a cup of coffee. He remembers pouring it and the next thing a nurse came and took it away from him and made him lay down on the couch. Diamond had gone to sleep standing up with the cup of coffee still in his hand. The next day, the only one Shirley recognized was Steve. She'd say, "There's my Baby." Diamond held her in his arms until the doctor pronounced her dead.

Most of the Hedrick's were at the hospital with Diamond when she died. Steve drove his dad home that night, he could barely make the road out he was crying so hard. When they got home, all Diamond's brothers and sisters were there. Daniel Stewart was there to comfort Diamond and Steve.

They had a beautiful funeral. Max Turpin did a wonderful job preaching. He was Shirley's first cousin. He is another preacher who loves to preach on the beautiful natural beauty around. He had just been up on the Cherohala Skyway and he told how with all this beauty how beautiful Heaven must be!

Daniel and Mickey Stewart did some inspirational preaching too. Diamond's sister Roma sang, "Going Up Home." Steve and Diamond had asked her in her beautiful voice to sing the song that was their favorite. Lennox and Sue also sang beautifully too. Most of Diamond's family are real good singers.

The next day, she was buried on one of the coldest days Diamond could ever remember. The wonderful ladies of Cedar Cliff cooked a wonderful meal for everyone at the Santeetlah Fire Hall. Diamond being the jokester he is, always enjoys funerals, because everyone gets together. He kind of treats them like a reunion.

Shirley was his wife of fifty years and meaning no disrespect, but being a jolly kind of fellow he couldn't help making the best of the worst occasion. In fact, Diamond's nephews were all pall bearers and they were worried about their cowboy boots and when they asked Diamond if the grave was on a steep hill. Diamond told them it was straight up in a broom sage field. He had them scared to death they would drop Shirley. It was a joke and he always has a lot of those!

When all got said and done, life was very lonely. Diamond missed Shirley and he needed to get back to his work. At night when all was quiet he would wake up, because he thought he heard her screaming for him. It was really nerve racking after four years living with her piercing screams, he had a hard time trusting all was well.

He had a lot of job offers but he was more than anxious to get away from the house. Everybody wanted the working man. He finally went back to work at his nephew Harvey's saw mill. He loves his nephew Harvey and Harvey was so glad Uncle Diamond was on the job.

The first day he went to work for Harvey he was being shown what to do and Diamond asked, "What do I do in my spare time?" Harvey told him he wouldn't have any spare time. Diamond being Diamond would quickly get caught up and he would go stand by Harvey watching him saw. He told Harvey never to holler at him, if you're not satisfied, just point to the little red truck at the bottom of the hill. Most folks around know all Diamond ever has are red vehicles, a Republican thing I guess.

Diamond was working hard and keeping his big place mowed in extremely hot weather. He was in denial that a storm was about to bust loose. It was on a Saturday and Diamond had worked all week at the sawmill. His field and yard needed mowing and he couldn't do it on Sunday, because most people in the mountains take the Sabbath day very serious. His Sister, Novella who lives next door, really would frown on that. On one of the hottest Saturdays, he got up early and mowed his big yard.

The yard is hard to mow, because it's on a hill and has to be mowed with a push mower. He was already sweating when he walked down to his field, where he mowed with his riding mower on the hottest part of the day. He was so determined to be ready to go back to work on Monday with all his mowing done. He got so hot that day, he started feeling very sick. The sweat was running down his back bone and puddling in his boots. As he walked back to the house to take a shower, he was feeling so nauseous and Diamond was ignoring his own warnings signals.

He had plans that evening to go to Donna and Andy Lewis' for dinner. He first headed out to Roma's house to see her and her family. When he got there, he found his little niece Jolie out on the dangerous cliff above the house scared and crying. Diamond was panicking as he hurried to get to his sweet little niece. The scared little two year old was so happy when he swept her up into his big strong arms. He was getting so very sick as he put the tiny girl on his shoulders and walked down to the chicken lot.

CHAPTER TWENTY FOUR

STROKE!!!

Roma had noticed a slurring of his speech and the corner of his mouth drooping down, but he told her it was an old bad tooth. He left Roma's to go to dinner, but not before everyone noticed his speech. Roma got so worried, she called Steve and told him when he saw his daddy to check to see if he was slurring his words. Steve met Diamond at the end of Andy and Donna's road on his way home. Steve said, "Dad, you are slurring your words!" Diamond told him, "Son, it's that old bad tooth."

Steve spent the night with Diamond that night. Diamond was sick all night. As sick as he was, Diamond knew not to wake Steve up, because he couldn't handle him worrying about him having just lost one parent. The thought of another sent him into a panic attack. Diamond did what he always did when he needed help, called Roma.

Roma came from Big Snowbird to Mill Town in lightning speed! She took one look at her big brother and knew he had to get to the hospital. Roma woke Steve and they headed out to the Bryson City hospital as fast as Steve could drive.

They did an MRI and the doctor saw a big clot above his left ear, "STROKE!" The doctor showed this to Diamond, saying he had had a stroke.

Roma put out the call to the prayer chain and soon the prayers were in the air everywhere! Scott Roper and Jim Postell came up to see him the next night. These are two preachers who have always been his best friends. Diamond seemed to be doing better and the therapist had him walking on his own pretty good. The doctor said if he made it through forty eight hours, he would be pretty much in the clear.

In the thirty eighth hour, Diamond was sound asleep when the big one hit! Diamond couldn't move or holler and the scariest thing was happening! He felt like he was dropping into a big dark hole going down, down, down. Being a real good Christian, he thought he was probably going to Hell and he kept waiting on the flames to get him. His only peace was that the Hell fire hadn't got him yet. It seemed like an eternity before anyone came, of course it probably wasn't, but to Diamond it was and he was terrified!

The nurse was finally able to wake him, and said, "Oh Lord, let me get some help!" The next thing Diamond knew, he was in a sea of frantic nurses and nurse's aides! It took all day to get admitted to the Asheville Hospital, where he could get the kind of help he needed.

Finally, they headed out with Diamond backwards in the ambulance, making him so much sicker. When he got to Asheville Hospital he was so sick and later the nurses would tell him they never saw anyone as sick. He was beginning to believe he would surely die and they really didn't think Diamond would live. He went through one bad time after another.

His mind would sometimes push him into troubled waters, because he would worry about himself. He couldn't move at all for days and couldn't talk. In all this, Diamond had good vital signs, good blood pressure, and the doctor said this was a stroke caused by stress.

Diamond had been through more stress than any man could handle. He had done so much trying to save his wife, being made to think they were saving her, he let them take all his savings. Even though she was diagnosed with stage four ovarian cancer. Diamond was led to believe she could make it. Now, he could look back and see how he should have maybe taken some time to rest and let the nurses take over. Diamond was not the kind of man to ever let her go through anything alone.

Now not talking was the hardest thing for Diamond and in his prayers he was sending up, he was asking the Lord, "please let me talk again!" Diamond has always had a gift for gab and he has always had his own language. When the speech therapist came in a few days, she thought this man was severely damaged. Luckily,

Roma was there when a very frustrated Diamond tried to tell her that's just the way he always said it! Roma told her you might as well forget trying to change his speech, because that's that ole' Snowbird talk! He has talked this way all his life, so the therapist gave up!

The next thing would be trying to get Diamond to move his limbs. He was then moved to a rehabilitation hospital. Steve had a good friend, Boxley that he worked out with, that was one of the best therapists. He met Diamond at the therapy room and the work started.

Every morning began the same, Diamond would get wheeled down to the swimming pool where he was so terrified. As they rolled him out into the pool the water made his bad leg immediately float up. He felt like he was going to drown. His bad leg that was floating was making his body sink like a box of rocks. The nurses of course were wearing bikinis, so he had to suck up all this nervousness and pretend to be brave.

Diamond promised Boxely he would be walking out of there when he left. Diamond went through a lot trying to get his body to cooperate with his brain. The frustration nearly did him in some days. Diamond also told Boxley someday he would return and show him how good he would be doing. In three months, when the nurse met him with a wheel chair to take him out to the car, Diamond told her, "Go get Boxley, I'm going to walk out of here!" With a walker and a whole lot of help, he walked out to his brother Loyd's SUV.

CHAPTER TWENTY FIVE

Un-happy Camper

Roma, Steve, and Loyd headed out to the Nursing Home with Diamond and he was a real unhappy camper as you might call it. Just knowing he had to go to a Nursing Home, he had a feeling of betrayal from his family. No matter how they assured him it was for his own good and only for therapy, he still felt betrayed. He kept remembering his words to Boxely, "I will come back some day and you will see me walking again!"

They were met by Assistant Supervisor, Sherry, who put Diamond's left arm around her neck to get him out of truck to put him in a wheel chair. Diamond kept holding on. Roma said, "You better turn her loose now!" Diamond said, "I don't want to turn her loose!" Sherry made Diamond feel good and made him feel welcome.

The one thing Diamond insisted on in the Nursing Home was the Fox News Channel. He told the Nursing Director, Donna Stevens, he had to have it. Donna having a father that lived and breathed Fox News understood. Her dad told her he wouldn't stay up there at all without Fox News either.

The Nursing Home was a much different atmosphere and Diamond was suddenly confused. He could hear the noises of the poor souls having their daily struggles. He thought he had Alzheimer's, so he called Donna and asked her, "Donna, do I have oldtimers?" She said, "No, what makes you ask a thing like that?" "Because you put me in an oldtimers unit. I'm surrounded by them." She laughed and said, "No you don't have Alzheimer's."

They didn't start immediately with Diamond's therapy like Boxley wanted them to. When they did, Diamond was all about getting everything going again. He had so much hope, but the young therapist they started him out with was so inexperienced. One day, when she was working with Diamond, he asked her about his right arm and if he would ever get the use of it back, it was still paralyzed. "You may never use that arm again," she told him.

Another therapist was over hearing these words. She immediately interrupted her. You don't ever tell a patient they may never use their arm again. You're taking away their hope! You don't ever take away their hope. The young therapist walked out and Jane Birchfield took over.

That was the beginning of a beautiful friendship and the best therapy Diamond would ever have. The first day, Jane took a group of them into another room, making a Christmas scene and Diamond's was so good they hung it in the therapy room. This was followed by singing Amazing Grace. Diamond loved her immediately. Back when Diamond sang, his uncles and aunts were always asking him to sing Amazing Grace for them.

A few years back Diamond's Uncle, Till Stewart, had called one morning and asked him to come sing Amazing Grace for him. Diamond went, because Till was real sick and he didn't want to let him down. Till thought of Diamond as his favorite nephew. He looked like Diamond's mommy's twin brother and they even sounded alike. It wasn't long after Diamond sang for him, he died. Diamond says that's the easiest he ever sang for anyone.

Diamond was and is a sweet man, and like most men, he fell so in love with all his nurses! I will tell you right now, no nurse could resist his beautiful sunny personality, including this CNA. His face would light up the darkest day. After telling him my name and seeing his name on the chart was Diamond Hedrick and all I could come out with is what every woman says when they meet him, "DIAMOND, now that's a pretty name!"

I really didn't think about the fact he was in a wheel chair. I had come to get his vitals as I stared down at his handsome face and sweet smile, I felt an instant gentleness. He had a very special glow, almost a ray of light around his head. I was instantly drawn to this sweet giant of a man.

After I told him who I was and that my grandparents were JD and Bertha Stratton, he told me he knew Grandma from many church meetings. She always got moved by the spirit so much she would get up and shout.

I can remember when I was very young going to an all-day singing and supper on the ground with Mamaw Stratton. All of a sudden, her neighbor jumps up filled with the spirit shouting and dancing all over the church. I'm feeling kind of scared and thought the woman had gone crazy. My grandmother, who was my security, until she jumped up also and went crazy too.

Diamond remembers when he would sing, she would hug him so tight and he loved that! She would pet him to death when he sang something that moved her and he definitely loved my Mamaw Stratton.

My grandpa, who was the mayor at one time, had helped him to get his water hooked up when he didn't have the money to pay the tap on fee. No wonder he really lit up at hearing they were my grandparents.

He also told me how he bought his first mobile home from my mother and had bought another one later. As we talked on, he said he had always been in love with my Aunt, Joyce, in high school. I was so fascinated with his stories. When I finished with his blood pressure I had to hurry off with this busy job I had taken on the week end. I left with so much curiosity about this very special man.

My husband had read in the paper where they needed CNAs for feeding patients on the weekend. Money was tight and I love feeding people. It was perfect for me. I had some really self fulfilment in the job I was hired to do. Feeding the poor folks that could not respond any other way but through their hunger. It was a job that required patience. I usually had two that I would go between with spoons of pureed foods, having to stop pretty often to help them with choking.

I usually got the patients that needed extra time and patience. Like a fellow who had AIDS, who was trying to give up. That was probably the most rewarding thing for me. He seemed to have excepted that no one out there cared and so he didn't. I convinced him in my most loving voice how I cared and I told him how good the food was going to help him to get well. I knew he didn't have long and I wanted him to feel loved. I talked to him about the country things, hunting, fishing, and the good old home cooking he would have someday.

At the end of each meal, everyone was amazed how much he would eat for me. This kind of work brought joy back into my life and gave me such a pride in loving people. It fueled my fire for the next parts of my life. That would be taking care of a very lost working man.

Nothing could have prepared me for Diamond. I couldn't wait to see him again and I quickly memorized where he was. Up and down the hall all day, handling the hardest things I had ever done in my life for some of the sweetest people in the world. The question that kept puzzling me was why Diamond was here. He wasn't helpless and he was so full of life, how could his family put him here? I had not even noticed the paralysis on his right side. I didn't know he was just there for therapy. I would soon find out about that family. I noticed the beautiful families visiting him, I knew he must be so loved and cared for.

Then one day, the medicine nurse, Shirley, stopped and asked me to take clean sheets to Diamond Hedrick's room and straighten up his bed. She said he has a lot of nice people come to visit with him at night. I was so happy to do that. We had a real nice visit and he was so sweet and worried to death I would bump my head on the hanging television. As I made his bed, I was ducking and dodging, and I looked for reasons to talk to Diamond. I offered to shave him, he said his brother would do that. Another job I had there was cutting hair, so I offered to cut his hair. He said his girl was coming Monday. Then all of a sudden, he asked me to do all these things when he realized it would bring me back in to him more.

He was always so sweet and always worrying about my poor hurting legs. The running up and down the long halls was taking its toll on me, even though it was just on the weekends. Diamond had this horse liniment he was trying out on all the nurses and he swore it would cure my legs. He was such a funny guy and all the nurses and aides loved him, including me.

This was a job that I felt I could not do, aides were fired all the time for simple mistakes and I had no confidence in some of the situations I ended up in. I went to my supervisor, Sherry, and told her I loved my job, but I just couldn't do it anymore. She begged me so to stay and she would make sure I didn't have to do the things that the other CNAs did, because I was only hired to feed. I decided to stay, but if I was needed I helped out. CNAs are angels and they go far beyond what you can imagine.

My next weekend, I checked to see what hall I had to work and found I had to go to the North hall that day. Knowing Diamond was on the South side, I went by his room before I clocked in and told him I probably wouldn't see him that day, because they needed me over on the North. He was very disappointed, but I didn't realize how much.

I was working right along that day and so busy when Sherry stopped me and said, "Marilyn I've got to put you back over there, Diamond Hedrick said if I didn't he was going home! I got to put you back, he says you are the best to help everybody." She says, "He loves you." I told her I loved him too. She said, "We all love Diamond."

All through my day I would look up and he would be there with a walker smiling. He really wasn't supposed to be walking alone, but some of the time he was venturing out on his own. I knew he was my favorite pet! When I would go home at night I would tell my husband all about my day. He would get so tired of hearing about Diamond, I could not help telling him about him.

It was Christmas time and our children were all living away in their own worlds. We had been struggling building our new house ourselves. Money was tight and the economy had just dropped off the map. America had been at war with Sadaam Hussain and having two sons in the military, I was in a deep depression. It seemed the only light I had was Diamond. One night, I needed to feel the real meaning of Christmas.

I clocked out after a long hard day and walked back down the hall to Diamond's room. He just thought I was saying good bye for the week. I took hold of the wheelchair as I told him, "I am going to take you down to see the Christmas lights. I just need to feel the spirit tonight."

At the home, they have an outdoor garden for the patients. They had it decorated so beautiful. It gave me such a beautiful feeling as I fed the poor helpless people in the dining hall. I would look out and think of how I would like to take Diamond to see it.

It was really too cold to take him outside, so I just stood behind him in front of the glass and looked out. I put my hands on his shoulders as we looked at the beautiful Christmas scene together. I finally took him back to his room. After parking his chair, I turned to him and he told me he loved me. I told him I do you too. I leaned down, hugged him, and he kissed me on the cheek.

I drove home that night and I felt so strange going around the curves at Topton as the music swelled through my car. I could have driven off one of the many cliffs and I didn't care.

As I got in bed, I had this very beautiful feeling that a spirit I had seen several months before suddenly made sense to me now. While I lay there in the dark, I had a feeling I might be somewhere else. The whole week I wondered about the strange feelings I had for this man that I still knew very little about. All I knew I could not wait until I got back to work.

Being married a very long time and having ups and downs, we had for the first time settled into building a new life on some land my parents gave us. How could I think of this man and what were my feelings? Where were these feelings taking me. He is like the father that I can be comfortable with. Looking so much like my dad and even saying things that my dad would say. Being able to trust that his sweetness wasn't going to change on me the way dad's did. No bomb was going to go off. So I loved him!

When I went back, I found the sweetest man waiting on me. He had something he had to tell me. He said, "You probably are going to think I'm crazy, but I had an experience. After you left me Sunday night you came back wearing the most beautiful white dress. Your hair came down on both sides and you called me by my name." He told me how he called out to me, "Merlan" and with that; he said that I disappeared (Diamond calls me "Merlen.") I'm realizing the connection to my feelings. I'm now believing in an out of body experience.

The thing he said that worried him so much was never seeing me again and it was causing him to put off going home. I told him I would come to see him at his house. That made all the difference, he was ready to go home. I didn't know how much longer I could work there, the job was taking its toll on my fifty-eight year old back and shoulders.

I wanted to give him something to remember me by. I found a print of a painting that I had done a long time ago and I brought it to him. He was thrilled. He had his friend, Tim Roberts, make a beautiful wormy chestnut frame for it. It is a picture that reminded me of my horse riding days that I found in National Geographic. When I painted it, I felt as free and powerful as the girl in the picture riding after the cattle with a flailing bull whip in the air. We all have our alter egos.

Diamond went home just down the hill and I kept on working. It was some of the coldest, snowy days of winter and It would have been hard to get home on some nights. Living at Andrews, I would be driving around the Topton curves, and was at the mercy of the icy patches of road.

We were expected to be there regardless. It is your responsibility to be there no matter what. After I spoke with Diamond on the phone, he told me not to drive on the roads that I could stay there at his house. He was glad for the company and that was when he started telling me all about the fascinating Hedrick's.

To make a long story short, I quit the Nursing Home and started helping Diamond. I would come and straighten his house and give him his showers. I also would cook several meals and put them in pouches for microwaving later. This I would do two or three times a week. I also spent a lot of time on the phone with the lonely man when I was at home.

We used to talk about so many subjects, especially about our father's logging stories. One night, we realized our fathers would have had to have worked together, because they had told us the same story. About an Indian fellow who was logging on this dry ridge, when he went down the hill to eat his lunch. He started holding his throat choking. He had eaten a big sweet potato and there was no water in that dry gulch. They asked what was wrong he said, "WATER!" Branch water a 'do!

We also started watching television over the phone. Diamond was never interested in anything but Fox News, football, and Atlanta Braves baseball. I can't stand Fox News and really never got into sports on TV, so I had Diamond watching "Say Yes To The Dress." He called it "Trying On Dresses." Steve called one night and asked his dad what he was doing, Diamond told him he was watching the show 'Trying On Dresses." Steve said, "What's wrong with you, Dad, are you crazy?!" Their favorite team was playing, The Green Bay Packers, and he never let on to me that it was so important to him.

I got Diamond interested in a lot zof things he never knew about. He had worked so hard and he was oblivious to the world I knew about. We had a lot of good conversations.

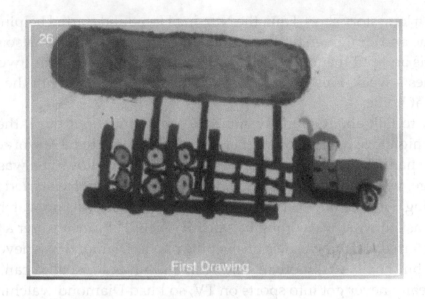

First Drawing

CHAPTER TWENTY SIX

Now What Are We Going To Do With This?

It was getting really hard on me to drive twenty five miles one way and back. Eventually to save money, Diamond came to live with us. This gave me extra money I needed to make it every month and I got to stay home and keep everything running smooth.

He had so many days that he wanted to go work at the saw mill, or wished he and Tim still had the log yard. Being handicapped has not been easy. He had never regained the use of his right arm, so all his purpose was gone. He was right handed and only having the use of his left hand has been a problem. Things like showering and picking himself up and off the commode has been the real challenge in his life. It is the most important things I do for him, besides cooking.

One day, it all almost came to an end. I had started wearing shoes that rocked to help my feet and I had even got some for Diamond. They made such a difference in the way I felt. My husband had recommended them, because they helped his feet and he had such benefits from wearing them at the furniture plant where he worked.

Diamond and I were gathering fire wood and Diamond unable to help, waited in the car while I climbed up a steep bank to throw some down. I started back down the bank in those rockers, when I rocked forward, losing my balance, running out of control, and slamming onto the top of the hood of the car. Diamond almost had a heart attack! This showed me the dangers, but that wasn't enough, because I loved those shoes.

One morning I was getting Diamond ready for his Chiropractor appointment and I had just put him on the commode. I was emptying my trash can and walking through my house when I rocked right up on a big dog kennel door in my living room we had for one of our more problem dogs. I was suddenly hung in the air and coming point blank down on one knee on our concert floor. Lucky to have my cell phone, I immediately called my sister, Nancy Curtis, for help. Hanging up I called my husband and he called for an ambulance.

I was in horror watching my knee deflate. The pain was more than I could handle and I could not bear to move. As suddenly as it deflated, my knee swelled three times its size before the ambulance came. It was my first, and hopefully last, time to ride in an ambulance. Getting to the hospital emergency room, I was told I broke my knee cap completely. It took a four hour surgery to put three long screws in my knee.

Diamond's first problem that day was being worried about Nancy seeing him with his pants down, so that was one day he managed to somehow get up off the toilet and pull his pants up by himself. Nancy saved Diamond that day, spending several hours counseling him. He was so sure his world was coming to an end and after Nancy dropped him off at Roma's, he went all to pieces. He sat up all night crying and worrying on her sofa.

The second day in the hospital, I was so worried about Diamond having to go to his sister Roma's house to stay. He nearly drove Roma and husband Hugh crazy, until they loaded him up and brought him from Snowbird to the Sylva Hospital to see me. Only he didn't want to just see me, he wanted to stay and take care of me. When I told him he couldn't stay, there wasn't enough room in the tiny hospital room, he broke down crying so pitifully. He was thinking he needed to take care of me the way he took care of Shirley.

They had to just about drag him screaming and I ended up crying seeing him that way. Next day I came home still having a lot of pain and with a big brace on my leg. Roma had to take Diamond to his house, because he insisted on being alone. He was being so stubborn and I was unable to comfort him on the phone. On about the third day, I loaded my crippled self into the truck with the help of a Rollator I had bought for Diamond sometime back, and drove across the mountain to Robbinsville to bring him back to our house. I still don't know how I did that now. I was crippled taking care of a very handicapped man.

I managed to do the laundry, cook meals, and assist Diamond, as well as take care of myself. My husband, Eddie had to work at the plant during the week and he wasn't too happy about me struggling while I was recuperating, but by now he had realized my commitment to Diamond.

I even started a procedure to sue the company that made those wonderful dangerous shoes, as they were being sued by other customers besides me. My case fell through, because of the kennel door being left open was our fault. North Carolina has some kind of a "no fault" law. That was an experience I can never forget. I am such a healthy and safe person, but that was a scary time in my life. I ended up taking my shoes back and getting a refund. Diamond's also had to go back because he was wetting all over the commode from rocking forward when he peed.

Being a creative person, I sometimes get depressed in the winter months, so I had started to paint again. I realized it might be something Diamond could do. He would be sitting there with no hope of working and nothing to do and he was very down most days. One day, I put paper and pencil down in front of him. I had this beautiful pineapple I set on the table in front of him, thinking he might try to draw this with his left hand. The first thing he did was draw a big cherry sogg at the top of the paper. I am thinking, now what are we going to do with this? The next thing the skid poles came down and a log truck went under! Then the log trucks started and Diamond drew everybody's log truck that had ever brought logs into the log yard. It filled him with so much purpose in his life! He drew what he knew best. I helped him with drawing the men in some of the logging pictures. When he started to draw farm scenes, I helped him out by drawing his horses and cows. He has now started drawing animals and people himself.

I always noticed what beautiful handwriting he had before the stroke. I can only imagine what his art would have been like if he had started before he had a stroke. He does everything, including his drawings, left handed now. He has all these little blocks of wood that help him with his art. They help hold his paper down and help him with the many lines he draws so straight. He has the tiniest little eraser that he has good control over, but when he loses it, he goes all to pieces! Now we have probably five really good ones, but he has to have that one! Then to help him make all those wheels he uses all these bottle caps and coins. He took this life to one more level. I still have to make him get up and walk around to take a break from his important work!

When he is working on something to share on Facebook, he gets so excited and is in a hurry to get it done! All his cousins have given him so much purpose and encouragement. The reason we are writing this book is so the memories of the brother's, sister's, and cousin's lives on Snowbird live on after we're all gone. They all give me stories, but nobody seems to remember like Diamond. He moved away, but he never forgot the home place his family grew up on Big Snowbird.

That's where his art comes into play. He draws on that big fat memory. To be the once owner of the greatest lumber yard and the hardest working man for so many years, he has always been a tender hearted teddy bear. He would run those old log loaders until he was cooked on those hot days. He had to be quick in his figuring and always being fair with the loggers. He certainly never imagined he would end up with art consuming his life. When we go places and he sees a man or men cutting trees or working, he gets depressed. He's always saying he wishes he could still do that. If he didn't have art he says, he might as well go on and be building his time. (That is his saying!)

Sometimes I ask him when something took place, Diamond's saying is "back when Snowbird was a little biddy branch." That means a long time ago. I'm really learning about the different signs in nature. One of the things Diamond always tells me about winter is if the squirrels build a lot of nests in the trees, we're going to have a lot of snow. It really seems to be right on cue the last few years. If the woolly worm has lines so far apart making it more black, we're going to have a bad winter.

Diamond had just finished a truck for Larry and Teresa Crisp, when their son, twenty-six years old, died very unexpected. They're still not sure what happened. The whole town loved Bart and Diamond remembers his daddy bringing him to the log yard when he was just a little boy. He was so good, so young, and handsome. Funerals like that are hard to go to, so we just drove up to the visitation and after seeing Dave Stewart, Teresa's dad, we gave him the picture. Larry and Teresa are having a hard time right now and this was such a heartfelt thing he was glad to do.

There have been a lot of logging friends who have died. Diamond draws their trucks and gives them to their daughters, sons, or wives. This makes Diamond feel so fulfilled. He never ceases to amaze me! He tackles the toughest pictures sometimes for benefits to help raise a little money.

In our home we have many animals: dogs, cats, and our sixteen year old squirrel, Junior, who just died. One of our dogs is a little Sheba Enue, Tiki, who adopted Diamond. He was a dog given to us by our oldest son, Rich, when he moved away from Andrews. Diamond needed Tiki, and Tiki needed Diamond and they are inseparable. Tiki sleeps in Diamond's room and until he goes to his bed, he sleeps at his feet. Now, Tiki should weigh in at around forty pounds, but because of the generous portions Diamond saves to feed the always starving Tiki, he probably weighs sixty or seventy pounds. That I'm sure came from the way Diamond's mommy always treated her little dog. She always gave him as good as she ate. Diamond always saves back a small portion for Tiki, who with Diamonds speech, he calls "Kiki." This is extra from his dog food.

26C Tiki.

I cook a lot of good food in this house, because of Diamond. He has inspired me to go beyond my culinary borders. I grew up with a mother that cooked Polk Salad, but I never gave that plant much thought. Any time we've seen it growing along the highways, Diamond always says, "there are no hungry people in the world." He grew up in a time when people were a lot hungrier and a stalk of Polk Salad didn't get wasted. He would pull up the tender shoots for his mommy and she would cook not only the green, but the pink root too. Now anytime we see Polk Salad, we get it.

Cooking it is a science too. You must first boil the plant and pour off the water. Then in a small amount of cooking oil, fry it, and beat an egg into it to smooth out the taste. Nothing is better for you and when you eat it, you notice several good things. Diamond always laugh and says it makes you shed off!

Some more greens that his mom had him gather that came in at the same time Polk did, were Crease, that grew in the fields wild. It was good a site, as he would say it. It was cooked just like the mustard they grew. Branch Lettuce was another good green that his mommy would always go with them to pick. It grew across the creek and a long way down the rail road tracks. Too far for them to venture out alone when they were little. They would at the same time gather Crows Foot to mix in with the Branch Lettuce they cut up together and poured hot fat back grease over it. Very good and when the children were old enough they would gladly go to pick these greens by themselves.

The mountains also have patches of natural wild onions, called Ramps. The first Sunday in May is when the families would go to their patches. People kept their patches their private little secrets. They treated their patches careful and replaced the disheveled ground. The onion is stinky, but very tasty when fried with potatoes or boiled.

Boys, such as Diamond, would eat them raw just to get thrown out of class. They were such a stinky bunch they would have to leave! Mary was always searching for the many wild things to eat and to feed her family and ramps were very good when she cooked them.

CHAPTER TWENTY SEVEN

Out of Smokes

Diamond's cousin, Jimtom Hedrick, is now a famous celebrity. Robbinsville has the famous Moonshiners from the television show "Moonshiners" living there and all are cousins of Diamond's. Jimtom had done a documentary show before, called "Mountain Talk." His sister, Pat Williams, appeared on it too. The show featured a lot of people of the area. They all have their own unique sound.

There were people from Yellow Creek, which is pronounced "Yeller Creek" or "Yaller Creek," and if you say "Yellow," somebody will quickly straighten you out. Those folks have their own certain way of talking. The upper end is different than the lower end. Diamond's wife was from middle Yellow Creek.

Diamond has that Snowbird dialect and Jimtom has a more of a twang than Diamond. Something that has left most southern areas, still flows in these hills like a song that never ends. It is the attraction that will keep you hanging on every word.

Jimtom's Skeeter

Jimtom has always been the most colorful of all. He was always the wild child. Diamond and his cousin were close in age and close in life. Diamond drew a picture of a vehicle that Jimtom called his "skeeter." He used it to haul pulpwood on. He always had a can of ether in the seat by his side in case he needed to give it a shot. Always going up Carver Hill, right before he got to the top, it would stall out. That's when he would use his can of ether.

One story Diamond remembers was on a cold night, when he and Shirley were living in Mill Town. The temperature was well below zero degrees. It was ten o'clock at night when Jimtom knocked on his door, getting him out of bed. He needed a ride home to Big Snowbird. Diamond begged him to spend the night with them, but he said he had to get home. Diamond had no problem taking his cousin home, he would do anything for Jim. Diamond was driving and just as he got to the swinging bridge, Jimtom said to pull over. The next thing you know, Jimtom climbs down to the frozen river and wades out to retrieve a tow sack. Now we all know what was in that sack, don't we? He offered some of the tow sack to Diamond, but Diamond refused. Diamond has a problem with toe sacks!

The most incredible story about a motorcycle wreck Jimtom had, has been told by everyone. Jimtom gave me the whole account and this is how it went. For $100.00 he bought a 1937 Harley Davidson Motorcycle back in 1962, from Gerald Buchanan.

It was on Halloween, when he picked up Billy Buchanan on Atoah and headed up Santeetlah, going through Joyce Kilmer and around the loop through Gold Mine Branch, up 129 through the Old Thunder Mountain Resort, then back into Robbinsville. They then headed home, stopping at the ESSO gas station at Bemis Lumber Company, where he filled up his tank with gas for thirty-three cents a gallon. It took one cent short of one dollar to fill his tank.

He then headed up the Snowbird Road, turning off onto Atoah Road taking Billy home. Getting back on the road, he continued on around the loop, and pulled into Robinson's Grocery Store. That's where he met up with Jerry Nelms and his girlfriend, Nelda Orr, who had her niece, Lavada, with her.

The two young men decided to race around the very curvy road and it was on! It was dusky dark when he hit the short little straight above Jasper Hedrick's barn and Jimtom's motorcycle was registering over 100 miles an hour, when he was suddenly confronted by headlights, and then BOOOOM! The Harley exploded on impact, with a car who pulled out to pass another car. In that car was Ed Nelms, the father of Jerry who was in this race. Jimtom remembers flying through the air, spiraling out of control, in a twisting frenzy. He thought, "If I ever hit the ground, I'm a dead nut! I'm really dead this time!" Just before he hit the big pile of rocks, he said to himself, "Lord help me." Jimtom says hitting the rock pile below, felt just like landing in a bed of cotton.

Jasper was carrying a pail of milk from the barn, when he looked up and saw Jimtom flying and twisting through the air, landing in the rocks below. He was hidden in the brush pile, where brothers Chad and Vance Headrick searched and found him with one of his legs turned backwards, and nearly cut off.

Jimtom wasn't wearing a helmet and he had a large split in his head. Somehow they got him loaded into Ed's car and headed out to the hospital at Andrews. He couldn't talk at all. All he could do was grunt, but he managed to smoke twenty cigarettes before arriving at the hospital. With all the worry, all he could think about was that he was out of smokes!

He had all the doctors working that night; Dr. Van Gorder, Dr.Rodda, and Dr. Blaylock. They all worked all night on the leg that was almost cut off with the bumper of Ed's car. The large split in his head took 157 stitches to close it up. It is such a mystery his skull wasn't split open, but he had no skull fractures.

Dr. Van Gorder told him they might have to take his leg off. Jimtom begged him to save it and I think the good Lord was listening. The Lord spared him that night and through the years, he has had many close calls. I was so sure I could tell you he was drinking, but he told me he was not drinking when this happened. I believe him 100%.

Diamond and Cousin Jimtom

Teds 83 rd Birthday

CHAPTER TWENTY EIGHT

Passions In Life

Diamond's brother, Ted, just had his eighty-third birthday. He still enjoys a full life. He is an inventor like his grandpa, Pose. He took a very old antique clock of Grandpa Pose's and made a beautiful clock from the inside workings from it. He is also a great wood carver and furniture maker. He makes wonderful toys for his grandchildren and great grandchildren. For the boys he's made log trucks and belt buckles, for the girls he's made dollhouses complete with furniture. Through the years, Ted has made ear rings out of walnuts and hickory nuts, and beautifully crafted jewelry boxes. He also had a display in the library in town with some of his woodcarvings.

He has made musical instruments too; a special banjo and guitar for grandson, Lance, who is a fine musician. He's made walking sticks for all the family and they are very beautifully carved. One of his walking sticks has Santeetlah Lake on it. He also has some sweet memories of their childhood.

He recalls a Sunday, when all the Hedrick's were home and they all were reading and doing different things. This day, Ted wasn't into any projects and he was so bored. He was sitting in a chair in the middle of the room with nothing but a clothespin in his hand. The cat came by with her tail in the air and for some unknown reason, Ted just clamped that clothespin on her tail. Well the silence suddenly erupted into the cat scratching, screaming, and shooting through the air like a lightning bolt around the walls, almost on the ceiling at times! Jasper thought the cat had gone mad and ran her out of the house. Ted just knew he was in trouble, but Jasper said in a calm kind of voice, "Well Son, I guess we won't be doing that again."

Ted really wasn't mischievous, he was quiet a serious thinker, and like his Dad and Grandpa Pose he was always studying things. He would go out to the Indian school and study an old churn drill that the Indians were drilling wells with.

It all started with him hearing the sound and he said he would have to go see what that was. When he got there, he was so impressed with this invention, he said one day he was going to build one himself. He never forgot about it and about thirty years later, he accomplished his dream.

Afterwards, he dug his own well and suddenly everybody wanted him to drill their wells. Ted realized he didn't want to go into the well drilling business. Knowing this, he put an end to that, so he tore it down, but still keeps it in pieces in his shop.

His newest project was building a wagon for a commercial ice cream maker for son, Eric. It has a 1915 John Deer motor. The wagon was handcrafted by Ted. All the wheels, axels, and spokes, were turned on a lathe and carved by Ted. Many painstaking hours went into it. His wife, Hester, sanded and polished it into a finish you can see yourself in.

The ice cream maker was mounted on it and it is ready to be loaded on a trailer and towed behind a 1950 Chevrolet truck to a location to sell ice cream. It will make twenty quarts at a time. It really is a piece of art. His son loved it and took it to Florida, where he lives. Ted decided to build another one for himself, only a smaller version.

Brother Ted's Ice Cream Wagon

Diamond probably could have done many workings like Ted, if he had only taken the time to develop them. He loved logging so much, that he got so involved in this trade he forgot to even think about another passion he might have in his life. He never knew he could ever draw, until everything was taken away. His work was his life and he had almost given up when he realized he could draw. His art gives him a purposeful life.

This has been as good for me as well. My own dad had so many problems in his life. PTSD that he struggled with in his life as a result of fighting in World War II. He had many head injuries and almost died. After many traumatic things he went through in the war, he came back pretty messed up. He was a very difficult man to give care to. My mother had years of abuse, just like all of my brothers and sisters, as well as myself.

I always tried to get my dad to take up art. He was the best at drawing animals for me when I was young. One day, I brought him pencils and art paper. I also got him a book of beautiful horses. I begged him to pick up the pencil. He never would. It has really haunted me that I could never even get him to try. If only he would have tried, he still had the use of his right hand. I have to think my dad is up there in Heaven, sending down messages to Diamond.

In all honesty Diamond looks so much like my Dad. It is one reason I love Diamond so much. It was always like a house fell on me when I met Diamond. I never could fully understand what happened when I met him. Whatever it was, it put together two people who needed a purpose in life. I always get the feeling I was put in my place from our folks and God. We both would have missed so much about this life, had the house not fall.

95

Steve Jordan   Marilyn Trull   Linda Schaffer   Diamond

29-A

CHAPTER TWENTY NINE

Young at Heart at the Pick &Grin

I've been taking him to The Pick & Grin in Andrews on most Saturday nights and he gets up and dances with all the pretty ladies. Mae Raxter and Donna Sellers are two that are very special women to him! They love him like I do. He has a lot of friends there, because most everyone who comes over are from Robbinsville. Diamond is the VIP all night and that suits him. He always needs a lot of Pettin'.

Diamond did not have dancing in his home when he was young. Religion didn't approve of dancing and even with the church hymns, the rhythm would take over the young boy's body. No matter how much his mommy would stop his jittering in church, he always had that clogging rhythm coming out of him. He also had a lot of other types of dancing he was good at, I'm sure. Music always tore him all to pieces!

You can see this even though he is partially paralyzed, at one time he must have been a site! He'll tell you that too. When the Blue Grass starts, it creates such excitement in his body, he can't help but give everything he's got to the dance.

Diamond uses a quad cane to walk, even though he had a therapist tell him he would never use anything but a walker. He is able to balance and support his tall musically motivated body.

With some of the greatest cloggers that you could ever see, Carolyn Snider is the best. She leads us into a dancing frenzy and Diamond is right there with us. Steve Jordan, who owns the music hall, always makes him the VIP all night. He's dubbed him "The Working Man," and sings the song "Working Man Blues" for Diamond. He laces Diamond's name all through the song. Making him swell up with so much pride and he does get the big head occasionally.

Steve has a daughter, Ally Jordan, who is an up and coming singer that we are predicting will be famous someday. She has the voice of an Angel! Last night, we walked in on a practice session where she was singing "I Told You So." If goose bumps are any indication, she will be famous very soon! I got them from the top of my head to my feet!

Sometimes when Diamond's bad arm will start shaking and jumping around, I have to take hold and steady it. Very often, one of the lady friends will forget he is handicapped and they get carried away jerking him around. I have to quickly step in and remind them he might fall. He has some really good friends that help with getting him in and out and up and down. Gary and Sharon Holloway along with Danny Hedrick and girlfriend, Barbara, who are all amazing dancers and are always looking out for Diamond.

I also have a real close friend, Martha Carpenter, who has become my right arm. If ever there was an angel, she's one. She is always watching to see if Diamond needs help, which really means she watches to see if I need help. I have never had a friend as good for me as Martha, she is also a good friend to my whole family. Sometimes she will load up some of the best suppers in a box and bring to us all the way from Robbinsville. She is one of the best cooks and I don't mind eating someone else's cooking especially Martha's. The meal that thrilled us all, was a meal of pinto beans, coleslaw, fried potatoes with onions, fatback, and cornbread. So wonderful!

Larry Queen is one of the really good cloggers and is always an inspiration, like Carolyn Snider is. I know without a doubt, if anything could bring Diamond's mobility back, it would be the dance. The Diamond that walks out on that dance floor is plugged in and ready to try anything! He lifts his left leg in the air and everyone goes wild.

He is such an inspiration to so many people. He loves being the center of attention and always has! The other night, a beautiful couple, Bill & Cheryl Suggs from Hayesville, came to The Pick &Grin, and Diamond noticed the man dances the way he used to dance. It brought back the memory of his style of dancing. Somehow after watching this man dance, I knew this was how Diamond danced before the stroke did its damage. I knew this before Diamond told me. Cheryl is so sweet and she loves to make Diamond feel like the dancer he was. Her husband is definitely what he hopes to be like again.

Sue Stiles, Gay Shuler, and Barb Davis are women who really get in there and pick up the pieces for the sometimes weeping Diamond. All these wonderful people are so loving and precious to Diamond.

I have a special friend, Eve Miranda, that is a spirited dancer like myself and together we can get the party started. We love to swing our scarves and sometimes our beads, and suddenly we become the life in the dance! I used to be one of the best dancers, like Diamond was. Because of all these friends, I find I am returning to the dance myself. Diamond brought back the dancing I never would have come back to if I hadn't needed it for his life. I now need it for my life again.

Raymond Norton and his wife, Leila, come dancing at the Pick-N-Grin, and also to Graham Care Nursing Home. He is a really unique man. He sometimes dresses up in an old woman costume for Halloween and other occasions. He clogs and he is one of the greatest. He and Leila are always having a lot of fun. He loves carving big bears for benefits.

He brings Diamond sorghum every year that really pleases him. As I drizzle it on biscuit bread, I hear Diamond saying more, more, more! I say, "We are going to taste it, not waste it." I also put it on his popcorn.

Diamond finds himself caught up in the drama of his good pal, Austin Beavers. He is always giving Austin his advice from many years of experience on just how he should treat his girlfriends. They always have a lot of man talking to do.

Sometimes these little boys like Ronnie Lee Seagert, age ten, want me to teach them the two step. I realize they are helping me instead, but who cares, we are all having such fun!

We are all so in love with little seven year old Eli Conley, who is really becoming a very good clogger and Diamond loves and enjoys him so much. These two little boys have touched Diamond's heart and he did paintings for both with themselves and himself in them. They both love Diamond the same way all the children love him.

Children just keep coming to be near him, he has that magnetic charm and everyone of all ages love to spend time with him. Brady Rogers and Dreydon Conley are cousins that are such sweet little boys. They are becoming real good dancers and we include them with us in the dancing. Dreydon almost has his dancing wings! I'm teaching him to get air born. A young lady named Brettleigh Miller is also dancing around with her unique style of clogging. She has such a beautiful spirit and we love her too.

Another place we really love to dance is where I met Diamond. It's called Graham Care now and the most wonderful people gather in the dining room to hear the Blue Grass played by the very talented musicians that donate their time. Diamond's friend, Bill Pruett, plays the banjo and he is one of the greatest. Buster Brooms plays the fiddle and he is a master! Pam Rogers, Jeanette Phillips, and Brenda Moody sing all the kinds of songs we love to dance to and also a lot of beautiful gospel music. A man who plays a big bass fiddle is Harvey Seay. A very nice man, Sammy Stiles carries it in for him. A brother of Buster, Jack Brooms, plays guitar and sings "The Working Man Blues" for Diamond. I just met Oliver Farley, who plays the guitar and sings too. They really make my feet beat out the many rhythms they play. They bring out my best and really bring out the shine in Diamond. Johnny Hensley plays mandolin and his wife, Mae comes to dance too. You cannot find better folks in the world. We like to think we help the sweet people that can no longer walk or dance remember their lives once, when they could dance. Diamond has a sweet cousin Dolly who has Alzheimers, who is having a struggle now. She still remembers a lot of the songs and sings along with Jeanette, Pam, and Brenda.

I have my sweet little Aunt Mary, who had a stroke, and at ninety years old she loves me to wheel her around the room where she gets to see some of her old friends. Diamond loved Mary from way back when she owned his favorite little Cafe, The Junaluska Grill. She was always my cute little sexy Aunt that always wore very cute outfits and had beautiful hair and nails. She still has all her jewery adornment every day. My own pretty mother Ruby loves to go with us on that day as well. She enjoys her visits with Mary and her sisters Vera and Edna while she's in Robbinsville. Momma loves to slow dance, but mostly likes Rock and Roll. I have found myself in some wonderful places with Diamond and sharing love with some really precious people. I love my life!

CHAPTER THIRTY

The Scary Times

Living in the same house with Diamond had some scary times. He would be fine one minute and unconscious the next, usually dropping straight down on our concrete floors. I would have to slap him to bring him back around. Sometimes I would hear a loud crash and I would never know what I would find when I opened his door. Usually a laceration on his head and blood everywhere.

One night, Diamond had a bad one and I took him into the clinic the next day. They checked his sugar level and it was fine. They sent him home and that night at the table he passed out. I brought him out of it again, and headed for the Murphy Hospital. After waiting in the ER for four hours, a doctor couldn't find anything to cause a blackout and had to send him home. We started to leave and at that moment it happened. I alerted the Doctor and he witnessed it. He said he had Epilepsy, so Diamond being the jokester he is, tells everyone he has Leprosy.

They then put him on a medicine called Dilantin, which made all the difference. We still had to go through several falls until we realized he didn't need sleeping pills. Having to get up to go to the bathroom at night, he would fall on the concrete again. These falls were because he was groggy and they resulted in him splitting his head and breaking his back. He didn't sleep anyway, so he got off the sleeping pills. They caused more damage in Diamond's case than they were worth. Diamond didn't sleep anyway and probably never will.

Through the years we have had to face several things. A big hernia on his navel was a much needed surgery and at same time he had his gallbladder taken out. This really helped his life.

When Diamond would see his Chiropractor who would see that big hernia that Diamond always told me was "Baby Diamond." He would ask him what that was. I spoke up, "Oh, that's a Baby Diamond!" The Chiropractor said he'd never heard of that term. Diamond laughed and said that was what he called it! I realized from then on, I better check out from now on what was a true story!

After Diamond had surgery, the Doctor said he just got to that in time. The per conium was leaching out poison into his intestines. Roma said everybody tried to for years to get him to get it fixed. Their mom and dad were always worried, but he wouldn't listen until I told him. He just needed someone to raise his bar a little in his life and I did.

The first day I decided to floss his teeth, I started with the few on the bottom and then started to floss the top when I was so surprised to realize he had no upper teeth! This man had been living all these years with hardly any teeth. Diamond lost his teeth because of Pyorrhea, it also caused his mommy to loose hers. Diamond was so embarrassed by this, really most people look terrible without teeth, but because he didn't have teeth for so long you couldn't tell.

We made an appointment with Dr. Kelly and set up appointments to get his bad teeth pulled and a set of dentures made. This has given him back what everyone takes for granted. Eating cashew nuts was something he loved and could eat again. Now, with that smile he can launch a thousand ships and he uses that smile too, on everyone. He is such a joyful person.

CHAPTER THIRTY ONE

Too Beautiful For Earth

We have all had a real heartbreak that my whole family has had to come to terms with our son Jonathan's little baby dying. I had seen a little verse on Face Book some months before he was to be born.

An angel from the book of life wrote down my baby's birth, then slowly turned the page, too beautiful for earth."

I was the most happy woman when I found out Jon and his girlfriend, Crystal, were having a baby boy. I even suggested his name, Easton. Waiting on him to get here, I could see him and I imagined holding him. The pregnancy was going so smooth and she was feeling better than ever. She had been so sick and this pregnancy had made her so healthy. Jon was excited and made a beautiful cradle for Baby Easton out of Ambrosia Maple. Jon's girlfriend has two little boys that we love in the same way we love our other grandchildren.

Desmond and Isaac & Elijah

102

Diamond and I were there when Jon took her to her last appointment. We kept the boys at their home out on the coast, while they headed out for what was her last checkup. After getting to the Doctor's Office, the nurses couldn't find a strong heartbeat. She was then rushed into the operating room to have an emergency C-section. It was a nightmare unfolding. Jon called and said it didn't look good for Easton. They had taken her into emergency and she was screaming! When he called me back it was the news, Easton didn't make it. I can still hear myself screaming. I got Diamond ready and along with the Boys, we headed out to the hospital.

Walking in and seeing them holding that precious angel was so disheartening. Then, when I looked at the most beautiful baby I'd ever seen, the little verse hit me. I told them, "Well that explains it. TOO BEAUTIFUL FOR EARTH!" We all held him and it was so hard to believe he wasn't breathing.

They did toxicology testing and examined him thoroughly and nothing was found. On the second day, I visited him alone, I knelt down, kissing him, telling him I loved him, and I would see him again soon.

The last two years have been a roller coaster. Their relationship fell apart, because she fell apart. This broke all our hearts, including Diamond's. He had taken on the role of being Grandpa too. He loved her like we did. She had even told him she wanted him to be her dad, because hers was out of the picture. Now it's over and we haven't seen her and the boys in over a year. We can only hope to see the daughter I once had and our grand boys. Jon has moved on and I hope he finds happiness, he sure does deserve it.

CHAPTER THIRTY TWO

Life Still Goes On

On May 2nd, life changed for Diamond. His son married the woman that Diamond has been praying for all his life. By Steve marrying Shannon, Diamond not only got a daughter, but also a Grandson. Shannon has a wonderful little son, Brayden, who is nine years old and plays soccer for his school in Asheville. He happens to be a really good player, which is such a blessing for Steve, who is a huge soccer fan. He and Diamond are already good buddies too and he spent part of his summer here in Andrews with Diamond.

There are a lot of good things that keep happening and we intend to focus on the positive. Diamond and I are back to dancing and he is socializing with all his friends. It's been a long winter, but we can see the light coming. Diamond is working on his art and I have all my tie-dye projects to sell. We are getting ready for Earth Week in Andrews. We have a lot to look forward to and a lot to try not to look back on. We've had a long cold winter, but we can feel the Spring coming.

Diamond's family are all still doing good. Sister, Minnie Jo, will be working in her yard that is always the most beautiful spot on earth. Her yard was once featured in Home And Garden magazine. She always has a show place. Her husband is a very good electrician, Earl Watts. They are a wonderful team and he helps Minnie Jo put things in place and tries to keep her from overdoing it.

Novella has been sick a lot, or she would be out more. Diamond remembers when she was her mom's right arm and she got to give him the hardest whooping's. She always said, "This is hurting me more than you." Diamond would tell her, "Then why don't you stop if it is hurting you so bad?" Diamond still thinks of her like his second mommy.

Loyd and wife, Marvadine, have a beautiful home and garden. They have a new great- grand daughter and they are having the best time being great-grandparents. They also enjoy football games having a Grandson, Auston Hedrick, who is a lineman and tackle for Robbinsville. A lot of excitement there with the Robbinsville Black Knights being the State 1-A Champions for 2014.

Another good mark for Pose and Frieda's offspring are the six players for the Black Knights this year. They are great- great -great grandsons, Austin and Toby Hedrick. Great great -great –great- grandsons Case, Wes, and Will Hopper. Another of the cousins who is great- great- great grandson of Pose and Frieda, is Landon Orr. These boys all played for Robbinsville this year as they went to the State Final Play-offs.

Another great- great-great granddaughter is Josie Cambell and she is one of the Black Knight Cheerleading squad who cheered them on. The Knights lost the last playoff game, but still a proud ending for 2015. Pose was born in 1886, 129 years before this came to be.

Roma has been putting her life as a tiny girl into play. Many days, you could look out at her daddy's meat house and there in the doorway she would be playing with her little dolls. Living the dream of being mommy. She only had the one daughter, but is living the dream of every great grandmother. She is totally involved in her great-grand children's lives. She and Hugh get them to their sports and they are always there when they need them. This is Roma's Cup of Tea. Her Pastor, Daniel Stewart, says Roma Atwell has watched more cartoons than anybody. We always know why she survived in the river that morning. She is one of the most important women in her family's life and church. Diamond always says Cedar Cliff Church couldn't have service without Roma. She would be so missed if she wasn't there. She is the HUB of the family and church.

Hugh is the Fire Chief and also a very busy man. He raises a big garden, enough to feed all their family around them. They still live on the land that Jasper provided. It is also home of their daughter, Rockanne, and her daughters, Lindsay and Amanda.

Amanda married Brandon Orr and they have children, Wade and Jolie. Rockanne also has two step daughters with her husband Kevin Sigmond, Ashley and Nicole.

Their children are also Roma and Hugh's Great Grandchildren. Ashley has two boys, Mason and Madden. Nicole has two girls, Lauren (Lulu) and Alonnah (Loni).

Diamond's brother, Lennox, is one of the greatest preachers. Diamond says he preaches love. He says God never asked him to preach on things people are arguing about. Never mentions the much too preached about politics. He preaches like their Uncle Gurley and prays like their Uncle Lesley.

Diamond says that Lennox is one of the best fly fisherman around. His health has been a challenge for some time, but he has that distinction of being a good one. Being able to put the line in and out of, and under bushes and rocks. He can hit any target, learning this from their Uncle Virgil. His wife Sue is a wonderful wife to the pastor and she raised a fine family and continues to make a beautiful home. She is an artist and has many of her beautiful paintings on their walls.

Ted, with wife Hester, are still staying busy in the workshop. After every project, Ted says he's through, but something is always pulling him back. He can never get through with his creativity. Diamond says he'll be six feet under before he will be through! The Hedrick legacy goes on, as a family they have done their ancestors proud.

My life consists of taking care of a very full house. All the cooking and cleaning up afterwards never stops. I was always cursed with doing dishes in my life, from the time I could reach the sink that's where I've been. Luckily, when I was a young girl I had a horse I could get away on. That went away when I got married at sixteen years old. I was a wife and mother for the first part of my life. I also was mother at times to other children besides ours. I had many children that I sometimes welcomed into our home from time to time. There were always many pets to take care of too.

Eddie Trull and I have made a life around loving our many animals. We have found ourselves with so many strays. I hate to use that word, but people keep throwing them away. Eddie has such a tender heart for the many unwanted babies and older pets that he brings home. I am just as bad, because I can never say no.

Eddie and I are both very interested in my newest project raising Koi. We have a couple of ponds and eventually I want to raise beautiful Butterfly Koi. Right now, I'm enjoying just feeding them from my hand and watching them grow. I sometimes get worried what will our children do with all this. When we die, what will happen to these sweet animals and fish? We will definitely have to cut back and eventually stop all this. The big dogs are getting harder to handle as we age. We need to scale back the size of our dogs.

Right now, I am so involved in taking care of Diamond. He is a whole other life for me. I have shared my art and creative side with him. I've made such a commitment to keeping him happy in his art. It is sometimes a conflict between my husband and him. I sometimes feel I am caught between a rock and a hard place. I somehow balance a life that both men are teetering in. I just keep praying God will keep me strong and keep me focusing on positive things.

Lately, I've been pushing the bar with Diamond. Last summer he entered three paintings in a local arts contest. Because he didn't win he was so upset, so this is why

I'm showing him no mercy. I am making sure instead of three we're entering as many as possible! His good friend and former therapist, Jane Birchfield, is inspiring him too. She says he needs to enter three in each category. There are about five categories that he could possibly enter, so a year from now look out Cherokee, Clay County Silver Arts! Diamond is loaded for bear! That of course means "He will be ready!"

A man that comes to the Pick & Grin, who has been a lifelong friend to Diamond, had a really special request for a picture he wanted Diamond to do. Diamond himself has been a Mason for many years and Billy Clark has been elected president of the Shriners in this area. Billy started out like everyone in Robbinsville in tough times. He ran away with the carnival when he was 15 years old. After a few years Billy Clark owned that carnival.

This was a really fun picture for Diamond to imagine, having gone to that carnival all his life. He sat for hours drawing all the rides and the people enjoying their carnival night. After He finished his vision, I came in and helped him paint, because he really draws so much better than he paints. I usually help him out there. This carnival scene really turned out nice and Billy loved it so much that he has some more ideas for pictures he wants Diamond to do. Billy also has raised a lot of money for something he and Diamond both have close to their hearts, and that is for children who are in need.

Billy built a beautiful home on the side of a mountain and he is making a special spot for the first Ferris wheel he first operated, when he was fifteen years old. He is doing this for his grand children. I hope someday to take Diamond up to photograph it, so he can draw it later. Who would have ever thought this working man from Big Snowbird could strike this blow with only his left hand!

Billy Clark's Carnival

The last seven years have been hard, but very rewarding. Diamond and I have done a lot of traveling. We've been to the beach five or six times to visit my son. We have met the most wonderful people when we've needed them most. Sometimes when I would be helping him walk down through the beach sand with a lot of clumps, he would become very unsteady. We would have it pretty well handled, but always some very sweet loving hands would come from out of the blue to help. You really realize what wonderful human beings there are in the world.

A really funny thing happened to Diamond one day. We had gone to Cheoah Point, picnicking and sunning. I was setting up our picnic and Diamond was walking down with his cane, when all of a sudden he tripped up. As he panicked, I saw the crazy fear in that big man's face! As I broke to run, the most beautiful woman in a red bikini stepped up and put her whole beautiful body into supporting Diamond. Well wouldn't you know, that scared man changed his frightened expression into a totally confident man.

If you are ever in Graham County and you head out to Big Snowbird, to get there you will go by the old log yard site. I want you to remember the man who had his working man dream there. Then as you go on around the winding road and you go up Carver Hill, that's where Cousin Jimtom had to throw the ether to his carburetor in his skeeter to make it on across. Go on around many sharp curves to turn left onto Snowbird Road, then go straight until you see a sign that says Sleepy Hollow Road. That is where the sweetest giant of a man was laid out for burial.

As you climb up the road to the top of Dobson Hill, you will see and hear some of the descendants of those sweet Hedrick cousins playing. The sweetest little sister Roma lives there with all her family around her. Leaving that curve you are soon where you turn down into Ted's workshop and home. This little stretch is where Jimtom's Harley exploded, sending him into the rock pile below. Jasper's barn is still there. It belongs to some lucky people that bought that wonderful place. A lot of what Jasper put together was sold off, like so many families that go a different way. Diamond always wishes he had taken what was offered to him. All families have to keep the peace and follow their hearts. In Diamonds heart, he will always be the WORKING MAN FROM BIG SNOWBIRD. The End.

About the Author

Marilyn Curtis Trull lives in Andrews N.C. with her husband Eddie Trull. They share their home and their lives with Diamond Hedrick. Marilyn's life is busy with taking care of Diamond who is partially paralyzed. She and Eddie have many dogs and cats that fill their lives. Marilyn's interest include dancing and her koi ponds. Listening to Diamonds stories through the years are why she wrote this book. She hopes it will inspire all people to reach out and touch the life of someone that might need help in their life. They might just find out they are rewarded in so many ways as she is with Diamond. Here is hoping that Diamond helps to inspire anyone struggling with not feeling productive in life to the point of giving up, find their way.

Printed in the United States
By Bookmasters